The Mental Game

Big thank you to Lina, Kim, and Ute as well as Katja, Oliver, Nadina, and Daniel

Daniel Memmert • Stefan König

THE MENTAL GAME

Cognitive Training, Creativity, and Game Intelligence in Handball

MEYER & MEYER SPORT

British Library of Cataloguing in Publication Data
A catalogue record for this book is available from the British Library
Original title: *Handballspiele werden im Kopf entschieden*, © 2022 by Meyer & Meyer Verlag

The Mental Game

Maidenhead: Meyer & Meyer Sport (UK) Ltd., 2024
ISBN: 978-1-78255-264-2

Aachen, Auckland, Beirut, Cairo, Cape Town, Dubai, Hägendorf, Hong Kong, Indianapolis, Maidenhead, Manila, New Delhi, Singapore, Sydney, Tehran, Vienna

Member of the World Sport Publishers' Association (WSPA), www.w-s-p-a.org
Printed by Print Consult GmbH, Munich, Germany
Printed in Slovakia

ISBN: 978-1-78255-264-2
Email: info@m-m-sports.com
www.thesportspublisher.com

CONTENTS

FOREWORD

At the Olympic Games in Japan in 2021, we enjoyed watching the different teams compete. I had hoped that our team would be one of them, of course. This would have been achieved through creative individual actions by outstanding individualists as well as through seemingly effortless combinations and fast and effective ball sequences by the whole team. The basis for these original solutions is cognitive components that are not put into the hand of any handball player, but which have to be honed through many hours of practice.

That was and is also the case with me. During my years with the Rhein-Neckar Löwen and Paris Saint-German, but of course also on the national team, my teammates and I have always very consistently trained things like perception, attention, and intelligent decisions. That's the only reason why I seem to be able to easily perceive goalkeepers accurately and attentively at the 7m penalty or on throws from my left-wing position and make the right throwing decision—or try something creative now and then; after all, a spin shot or a lob are exactly the things that our spectators and adherents want to see.

With The Mental Game, coaches are given the opportunity to devote themselves intensively to the all-too-often neglected cognitive skills. The importance of the head for ambitious A-youth teams up to the regional league or even the professional level is indisputable. I have always attributed special importance to cognitive training, no matter where I am playing. Until today, however, coaches in Germany have always had to fall back on their own knowledge or had to painstakingly search for references and game forms on cognition in handball in relevant handball magazines. This book closes the gap. With numerous game forms on the six cognitive abilities–anticipation, perception, attention, game intelligence, creativity, and working memory–it is now possible to quickly and easily get ideas for daily training practice.

I hope that this book will help to bring cognitive competencies, which have received the least attention in the training process up to now, back into focus. The greatest potential lies dormant in the cognitive area; we should learn to use it as effectively as possible. This applies to every handball player, from the district class to the national team.

Uwe Gensheimer

Captain of the German national handball team

ACKNOWLEDGMENTS

We would like to thank numerous colleagues with whom we have had the privilege of researching and publishing on the topic of cognition in recent years and whose ideas we have integrated (cited, of course) (alphabetically): Dr. Philip Furley, Prof. Dr. Norbert Hagemann, Jun-Prof. Dr. Stefanie Klatt, Dr. Timo Klein-Soetebier, Prof. Dr. Benjamin Noël, Prof. Dr. Klaus Roth, Dr. Sebastian Schwab, and Prof. Dr. Matthias Weigelt. Of course, we also say thank you to all our students who made valuable contributions to the individual sub-studies.

A research program rarely results from the ideas of one individual, but rather from the collective thoughts of many in a pleasant atmosphere. In addition, we would like to thank all those who critically proofread parts of the book in advance. These are in particular (alphabetically) Prof. Dr. Norbert Hagemann, Prof. Dr. Oliver Höner, Dr. Carina Kreitz, PD Dr. Florian Loffing, Prof. Dr. Matthias Weigelt as well as Elke Weyermann, M. Sc. We would like to thank Marina Gabriel, Erika Graf, and Linnea Schneider for their help in selecting the games, creating the illustrations, and providing diverse feedback. Dr. Philip Furley provided us with central support throughout the process, which we greatly appreciate.

Daniel Memmert and Stefan König

MIRALBET
BGV
VERSICHERUNGEN
ADMIRAL
DURAVIT

1 HANDBALL MATCHES ARE DECIDED IN THE HEAD ...

Andy Schmid, Uwe Gensheimer, and Domagoj Duvnjak seem to effortlessly manage to conjure up unusual–but also technical and tactical–best solutions on the field in extremely complex situations. Successful coaches, and often even other players, mention these exceptional players' mental speed, saying that "the head is important," or "they are very quick in the head," or "they are intelligent players."

Coach Nikolaj Jacobsen (current coach of the Danish national team) also knows about these qualities: "Andy Schmid is our thinker and driver. He is very important for the team. Without him, we don't think" (www.stuttgarter-nachrichten.de/inhalt.schweizer-schmid-ist-weltklasse-der-lionel-messi-des-handballs.1058b099-a753-4396-b557-eb3ab86108c9.html).

Good examples are statements in handball magazines that talk about speed of action and handball textbooks that repeatedly emphasize that handball games are decided in the mind (Wagner, Finkenzeller, Würth, & Von Duvillard, 2014; Weigel, 2018). In addition, a whole series of studies are described in sports science journals, which underline the special importance of the coupling of perceptual skills and reaction or action speed (i.e., reactive agility).

"A physical advantage won't get you much further in the game. It's more important to make quick decisions in your head." –Uwe Gensheimer, national handball player

---

"But apart from that, there are various players in the men's and women's game from whom I take individual aspects as a role model and want to emulate them. These are things like: Decision-making, finding the right gaps in the attack." –Emily Bölk, national handball player

---

"With every win, your self-confidence increases, which enables you to determine the game yourself and to follow through with our coach's tactical instructions." –Finn Lemke, national handball player

Agility definition (Friedrich, 2005, p. 143)

"Especially in sports games, it is essential to implement technical and tactical actions successfully according to the situation. The level of action speed is defined by the total time required for the cognitive processes (mental speed) and the motor solution of the active task."

Common to all terms and approaches is that the mind and thus cognitive abilities seem to play a fundamental role in handball and other sports games (see also Thienes, 2020).

In sport, cognition is the problem-solving process necessary for generating adequate solutions in specific situations. To this end, this book presents a model of the processes of human decision-making. Cognitive abilities such as anticipation, perception, memory, or attention that contribute to creativity are described. This also includes game intelligence (i.e., the selection of the best decision). In a more general sense, cognition can also add will, moods, and emotions. In training, it can now be a matter of practicing all these abilities individually or in combination, making them available in the memory.

Handball occupies a high status in sports science in general. There are many research results on this topic from different disciplines (e.g., biomechanics: Rojas, Gutiérrez-Davila, Ortega, Campos, & Párraga, 2012; handedness: Loffing, Sölter, Hagemann, & Strauss, 2015; diagnostics: Raab, Zastrow, & Häger, 2008; conditioning: Madou, 2020; Pietro, 2018; motivation & dropout: Sarrazin, Vallerand, Guillet, Pelletier, & Cury, 2002; motor skills: Krawczyk, Bodasinski, Bodasinska, & Slupczynski, 2018; psychology: Kajtna, Vuleta, Pori, Justin, & Pori, 2012; Ohlert & Kleinert, 2015; Strykalenko, Shalar, Huzar, Voloshinov, Yuskiv, Silvestrova, & Holenko, 2020; referees: Debanne, 2014; Morillo, Reigal, Hernández-Mendo, Montaña, & Morales-Sánchez, 2017; talent: Schorer, Faber, Koopmann, Büsch, & Baker, 2020; sleep: Jarraya, Jarraya, Chtourou, Souissi, & Chamari, 2013; Schorer, Heibült, Wilson, & Loffing, 2021; time out: Gutiérrez-Aguilar, Montoya-Fernández, Fernández-Romero, & Saavedra-García, 2016; and world state analyses: Lames, Dreckmann, & Görsdorf, 2010; Hansen, Sanz-Lopez, Whiteley, Popovic, Ahmed, & Cardinale, 2017).

Of particular relevance for this book, however, are the areas of perception, anticipation, attention, creativity, game intelligence, and working memory, with a sufficient number of publications available only for the first three cognitions. Nevertheless, even from these studies not all scientific results have been transferred into practice. This can be seen in the fact that people are amazed when Rolf Brack teaches game forms for perception and situation-appropriate decision-making, in which four different colors (different teams in relation to four goals) play a role, or when he combines brainteasers with motor responses in his training. This is considered revolutionary, but much more is possible in this respect.

For the first time, scientifically founded statements about cognitive training in handball are provided in this book. The content, methods, diagnostics, and practical aspects of the cognitive training are also discussed.

The first part of the book presents the basics of cognitive training:

- What are the key factors that can be trained?
- What kind of models are available?
- What kind of evidence is available?

In addition, these findings are linked to coaching practice. With a single word, coaches can vary the players' focus of attention. Maximum attention is needed in situations where variability and creativity are required. If, on the other hand, movements and actions are to be anticipated, or attention is required for specific events, then a narrow focus of awareness can help. Over the past 15 years, many studies have been conducted, and the role of the working memory in such situations is now apparent.

The possible cognitive diagnostics are subdivided into tests on elementary cognitions in the laboratory, or the field on the underlying model. To determine, for example, how significant the attention focus of a player is, his attention window can accurately be determined in the laboratory.

In very extensive studies with top athletes, there are also attention tests that were developed to precisely specify the attention window of an athlete. In addition, there are also diagnostic tools that can be used in practice. It is possible to see, for example, how players can shield themselves from interfering variables, how distributed or selected their attention is, and how well they are able to focus. There are now numerous test procedures to assess these situations. At the same time, there are established game-related tests in the field (indoor or outdoor) that can be used to evaluate the athletes' skills in finding gaps, and releasing in space. These form a basic tactical foundation and are important not only in handball, but also in other sports games.

In chapter 5, training examples are given in the form of game, competition, and exercise forms for cognitive training. Coaches and clubs must be made even more aware that attention and creativity can be trained along with anticipation and perception. For this purpose, numerous examples are presented that are structured according to the content model of cognitive training, which is described in the next chapter.

2 DEFINITION AND RELEVANCE OF COGNITIONS

What exactly is cognition, or cognitive processes, from a scientific perspective?

The use of the term cognition has a long tradition, ranging from Tolman to Hebb and Neisser to Gazzaniga—all famous scientists. At this point, no precise overview of the existing diversity of definitions is presented (e.g., for an overview in psychology, Neisser, 2014; for an overview in sport, Memmert, 2004a). In contrast to purely physiological, neuronal, and precognitive processes, Roth and Menzel (2001, p. 539) characterize mental performance through six cognitive processes:

1. Integrative, often multisensory and experience-based processes of perception.
2. Processes that involve recognizing individual events and categorizing or classifying objects, people, and events.
3. Processes that take place either consciously or unconsciously based on internal representations (e.g., models, imaginations, maps, hypotheses).
4. Processes that involve an experience-controlled change in perception, leading to changeable processing strategies.

5. Processes that require or include attention, expectations, and active exploration of the stimulus situation.

6. Mental activities.

In general, cognition is simply defined as those higher mental functions and processes necessary to generate appropriate solutions in certain situations in given environments.

The significance of cognitive abilities in sport is not conclusively clarified and is currently the subject of an intensive discussion. This also extends to psychology (for an overview, see Simons, et al. 2016; Hambrick, Burgoyne, & Oswald, 2019). However, findings from general psychology increasingly support the idea that fluid intelligence and creativity are influenced by various elementary and cognitive processes (e.g., inhibition; Benedek, Jauk, Sommer, Arendasy, & Neubauer, 2014).

Thus, we are in an exciting phase for both sports science and sports practice. For example, while one research group has been presenting data for years showing that training the working memory capacity is positively related to various cognitive performances (cf. Klingberg, 2010), another research group has not been able to confirm these relationships with any regularity (cf. Owen et al., 2010). In principle, the question is always whether the training of an elementary cognition leads to transfer effects on other domain-specific performances.

Executive Functions

An actual model for cognition from psychology (Alvarez & Emory, 2006), which is also occasionally used in sports psychology as a basis for research programs, describes the control and regulation of specific cognitive processes in humans. These executive functions (EF) regulate goal-oriented, future-oriented behavior (Friedman, 2006) (i.e., processes such as decision-making). EF are further divided into core EF (CEF) and higher-level EF (HEF). CEF is formerly characterized by working memory, cognitive flexibility, and inhibitory processes, while HEF involves problem-solving and argumentation strategies, as well as planning processes (Diamond, 2013).

These abilities develop with age as they depend on different prefrontal brain structures. The neuronal structure underlying the HEFs is the prefrontal cortex. It matures slowly and lasts in development; full capacity is reached between 20 and 29 years (Luciana, 2005). CEFs, on the other hand, develop earlier in life, mostly before early adolescence (Crone, 2006). In this book, both form the basis of the models and findings presented. The CEFs are associated with working memory, tracking of objects, and inhibition processes using the perception capacities and flexibility of the attention window, since these develop earlier than the HEFs and thus could be a key indicator in the early development process of players. The HEFs address anticipation, game intelligence, and game creativity, which can also be profitably trained in later training phases.

In two sports science meta-analyses (Voss, et al., 2010; Scharfen & Memmert, 2019a), small to medium effects of essential cognitive performance in experts could be demonstrated, which indicates superior (basal) cognitive abilities of elite athletes. Individual working groups have also discovered that sports experts (especially professional handball players) seem to possess outstanding basal cognitive skills (Vestberg et al., 2012; Verburgh et al., 2016). However, the number of studies is still too small, the methodological quality is critical, and there are also some published studies that have not proven any connections (cf. Furley, Schul, & Memmert, 2017).

Finally, a cross-sectional study by Scharfen and Memmert (2019b) of highly talented young soccer players demonstrates that, for example, a significant attention window can be advantageous for more complex motor skills, such as dribbling. In addition, a lower reduction in individual perceptual load indicates a higher sprint speed and a better working memory affects more precise ball control and dribbling ability. These findings will soon need to be replicated, particularly in larger samples.

A systematic overview of commercial cognitive training programs and their impact on sport practices (Harris, Wilson, & Vine, 2018) shows that many questions remain unanswered and need to be clarified in follow-up studies. Nevertheless, we firmly believe that we must begin to train cognitive skills in practice even before science has answered all of the questions from A to Z. In many places, a little courage is needed, and in other places, humility and restraint is required. The dilemma of general, unspecific domain cognition can be illustrated best by the metaphor of a transport vehicle such as a car or an aircraft.

On the one hand, regardless of whether the vehicle is a sports car, tractor, or truck, the larger the engine (unspecific, since motors are also used in many machines), the faster you will drive. The better the technology (even non-specific), the safer you will be on the road. On the other hand, different means of transport also have different requirement profiles. For example, an aircraft needs different tires and an entirely different engine. However, in the space or automotive industry, the mixture of rubber materials that should be used for the tires of airplanes or cars is already known and perfected, but this cannot be said for cognitive processes in complex sports yet.

Cognition in Analogy to Lactate

Good endurance (illustrated by the metabolic degradation product lactate) counteracts early fatigue, regardless of the type of sport (e.g., handball, athletics, weight training). This can be demonstrated, for example, in a reduced period of time for recovery between training sessions or between training sets. In a classic study by Spencer and Gastin (2001), it was possible to prove that even in the 200-meter sprint, which is well under 30 seconds, there nevertheless is a part of almost 30% of an aerobic metabolism. Thus, lactate can be described as an unspecific (i.e., independent of movement/sport) parameter (analogous to unspecific memory and attention processes) for the aerobic running performance of an athlete.

When lactate was first investigated in soccer 40 years ago (Ekblom, 1986), many were skeptic of its science and practice. Today, lactate diagnostics is an integral part of training control, and its targeted and systematic use has become indispensable in youth and professional soccer and handball.

If we transfer the example of the engine to a sport, this can mean that an excellent handball player can benefit from both a broad focus of attention and a large working memory, which can be acquired through a talent selection process or a lot of experience in handball situations. This brings such an excellent handball player to the position of making more efficient decisions, since he is able to integrate more players and opponents into the decision-making process.

On the other hand, it is also reasonable that excellent handball players only score well in attention, working memory, and field performance tests (including talent selection processes) because they have other talents or abilities that influence their game performance to a very high degree. For example, this could be high ambition, high motivation, or a high willingness to make an effort.

It is difficult to estimate which of the two positions will provide empirical support in the future. Perhaps both will have their justification, and the truth will be in between. For this reason, it is recommended to simultaneously be courageous and humble. In the following chapters, further findings from movement science and sports psychology on elementary cognitions are discussed. And this is no small thing.

79
nH
HOTELS
Cocoa
from
Ghana
RED-RAG

3 COGNITION IN HANDBALL

As it applies to sports (e.g., handball), table 1 shows elementary cognition from a biopsychological, evolutionary, developmental, and cognitive perspective, which can loosely be linked to necessary tactical competences, and in turn be of fundamental importance in various sports.

Table 1 Elementary cognition with regard to various sub-disciplines that could serve as a cognitive basis for mastering basic tactical tasks in sports games (Memmert, 2004 a, p. 137)

Tasks	Operational-ization	Biopsychology	Evolution Psychology	Development Psychology	Cognitive Sciences
Attacking the goal	Head for time and location	Targeted orientation performance		Object search	Orientation towards a target
Moving ball to goal	Distance estimation	Assessments of directions		Distance coding	Distance differentiation
Using gaps	Spatial decision	Localization of objects		Object-related perception	Object differentiation
Feinting	Ball avoidance	Stimulus-related reactions	Stimulus-related reactions	Concrete reactions	Stimulus-related reactions
Interplay	Adequate pass	Temporal-spatial structure of sensations	Stimulus-related reactions		Visual location/ orientation
Creating a majority	Outplay	Spatial imagination	Spatial reactions	Locations reactions	Location reactions
Offering and orienting	Spatial orientation	Cognitive Maps	Spatial orientation	Spatial cognition	Spatial cognition

In addition to such basal cognition as using gaps (see chapter 4), more complex cognitive abilities have also been discussed in sports science for many years. Based on the paradigms of psychology, a model of the process of human decision-making was developed (Memmert, 2013, 2017a, b; Memmert & Roth 2003; Roth & Hossner 1999). This model includes cognitive abilities such as anticipation, perception, attention, creativity, game intelligence, and memory (see figure 1) and was primarily developed for games since creativity or attention in swimming or track and field are not as central as they are in handball. In games, many different possible solutions are needed in order to succeed.

Handball players, in particular, want to anticipate a situation based on previous experiences stored in their memory, so that specific environmental factors are perceived and taken into account either consciously or unconsciously. After the conscious or often unconscious mental generation of a certain number of solutions available in the space of their memory, a creative idea, or the best resolution, is finally selected. This can be illustrated by the following sequence from the European Championship match between the French women and the Slovenians (2018).

Practical Example of Cognitions in World-Class Handball
(see https://www.youtube.com/watch?v=st1Bwu6Rb5g)

After a blocked goal throw by the Slovenians, the French goalkeeper notices a free teammate and plays to her. No. 7 bounces at high speed towards the center line. With two quick passes the midfield is bridged and No. 7 is able to pass intelligently to No. 21 at about 12 meters at the right moment. This pass is timed so that No. 21 can receive it at full speed. Player No. 7 benefits from her working memory, in which it is stored that there is always another player running in the left lane. No. 21 can therefore throw almost unhindered. Further creative solutions (e.g., a jump pass to the right wing) would be possible with a slightly different defense.

In the following, the cognitive factors anticipation, perception, attention, game intelligence, creativity, and memory processes responsible for the successful solution of tactical situations in tennis are emphasized (figure 1). The representation of the individual psychological processes follows a widely accepted temporal sequence, whereby not all perceptive cognitive phases have to be passed through necessarily in the real context. All six cognitions are also investigated in numerous scientific handball studies in recent years (Kiss & Balogh, 2019) and are considered particularly relevant for practice (see the review article by Wagner et al., 2014).necessarily in the real context. All six cognitions are also investigated in numerous scientific handball studies in recent years (Kiss & Balogh, 2019) and are considered particularly relevant for practice (see the review article by Wagner et al., 2014).

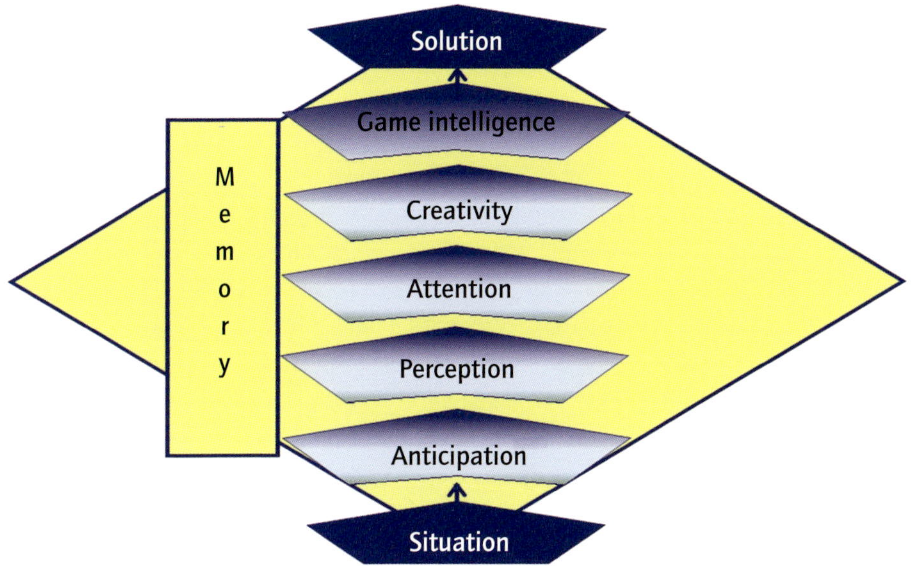

Figure 1 Overview of the central cognitive performance factors underlying all actions in handball (Memmert, 2013). All perceptive cognitive phases do not have to be passed through necessarily in order to generate handball-specific situation solutions.

Anticipation

Anticipation is significant in many sports (Hagemann & Loffing, 2013; Williams & Jackson, 2019), but especially in handball (Loffing & Cañal-Bruland, 2017). In this sport, more studies have been conducted on anticipation when compared to all other five cognitions. For example, in handball, the time to save a 7-meter is so short that goalkeepers need to anticipate the direction of the ball before or at the moment the ball is thrown. Therefore, research in sports has differentially addressed the corresponding latent or overt cue stimuli of the players (e.g., shooter or goalkeeper) that can be used to anticipate the intentions of the opposing athletes to act (Mann, Schaefers, & Cañal-Bruland, 2014; see Loffing, Cañal-Bruland, & Hagemann, 2014, for a summary).

The research group around Schorer has presented an impressive number of studies in handball in recent years. It is noticeable that most scientists use 7-meter situations as the study situation and choose the goalkeeper's perspective. In various studies, the shoulder area and the throwing arm of the goalkeeper were identified as regions relevant for anticipation, less frequently the head, the upper body, or the opposite arm (figure 2). Unlike novices, experienced goalkeepers overall tend to rely on a more global perceptual strategy, integrating cues from different distal and proximal body regions (Loffing & Cañal-Bruland, 2017; Schorer, Panten, Neugebauer, & Loffing, 2018). Current research is addressing contextual or situational information (including field position and previous events) of cue stimuli external to motor movements that can be used to anticipate opponent action intentions. These include, for example, the quality of play of teammates (Magnaguagno & Hossner, 2020) and opponent action preferences (Mann et al., 2014).

Figure 2 Summary of studies on anticipation-relevant regions from the perspective of the handball goalkeeper (selection).

Numerous studies have also addressed the training of anticipation in sports games (for a good overview, Loffing, Hagemann & Farrow, 2017) and handball (Klein & Späte, 1989; Duell, Eyßer & Späte, 1981; Brack & Bauer, 2020, 2019). Usually, sport-specific, anticipation-relevant information is taught via film-based simulations or, much less frequently, via on-site training sessions with a live model. Results specifically from handball (including, Alhosseini, Safavi, & Namazi, 2015; Schorer, Panten, Neugebauer, & Loffing, 2018) can be used to design training programs as well as test whether they can be used to improve anticipation in athletes, especially beginners (e.g., Abernethy, Schorer, Jackson, & Hagemann, 2012; Alsharji & Wade, 2016; Bideau, Multon, Kulpa, Fradet, Arnaldi, & Delamarche, 2004; Bourne, Bennett, Hayes, Smeeton, & Williams, 2013; Cocić, Vaci, Prieger, & Bilalić, 2020; Gredin, Bishop, Williams, & Broadbent, 2020; Gutierrez-Davila, Rojas, Ortega, Campos, & Parraga, 2011).

A particularly important question is how to promote anticipation through different training methods (see Farrow & Abernethy, 2002; Williams, Ward & Chapman, 2003). Which form of instruction is the most promising for facilitating the learning of anticipation?

Memmert et al. (2009) tested different training conditions (from easy to hard, context interference conditions, and feedback effects) on the improvement of anticipation. Variable, randomized training with little feedback is shown to be beneficial. Other studies have evaluated explicit, implicit, and controlled exploratory learning. Jackson and Farrow (2005) present an overview of the different approaches to training anticipation and discuss the potential benefits of implicit learning methods.

In addition, it has been demonstrated that sport-specific anticipation can be developed without the need for a direct link between perception and motor skills (i.e., sport-specific movement technique) (Williams, Ward, Smeeton & Allen, 2004). This allows for perceptual training under laboratory conditions for injured athletes, athletes traveling to the competition site, or athletes who would like to conduct additional independent training at home.

Hagemann and Memmert (2006) were also able to show that verbal instructions and appropriate instruction within a real field-based training program improved anticipation performance as much as a video-based laboratory program.

Example: Effectiveness of Anticipation Training in the Field

A training study by Hagemann and Memmert (2006) will be used as an example to illustrate that field-based anticipation training can also lead to an improvement in specific anticipation abilities, compared to laboratory-based anticipation training (using video clips). The field-based training intervention was based on findings of the anticipation ability in badminton (Abernethy & Russell, 1987). All players were given tasks to predict the direction of an opponent's shot. The anticipation performance was recorded before and after the intervention and in a later transfer test, with an established badminton-specific anticipation test (Abernethy & Russell, 1987). The results of the field-based intervention show that it is possible to train the anticipation of overhead strokes in badminton. This is unaffected by the trainer and was confirmed by the fact that all participants of the various training groups, from two different universities (Heidelberg and Münster), improved their anticipatory performance. The reason why anticipation skills of the field-based intervention are slightly reduced, compared to those of the laboratory-based intervention, may be due to most players being beginners since the exercises were usually performed with a partner from the same training group. The analysis of the video clips with regard to the expertise of the test persons explicitly shows this. The participants in the laboratory-based intervention, the only group to receive video material with Bundesliga players, usually show a successful adaptation by anticipating the strokes of Bundesliga players, but not those of novices or regional league players. This confirms the importance of using experts as role models in the training process, especially considering that it is generally more difficult to predict the direction of Bundesliga players.

The use of instructions thus enables coaches to direct the athletes' attention to anticipation-relevant regions that contain the most essential movement characteristics.

Perception

Perceptual abilities also play a dominant role in sport (Williams, Davids, & Williams, 1999), especially in handball (Lidor, Argov & Daniel, 1998). Handball games are often characterized by complex situations in which appropriate reactions have to be evoked in the shortest possible time. The (correct) perception and use of information is therefore crucial for a successful action planning and execution, which is why outstanding athletes differ from average athletes in this ability (Bourne, Bennett, Hayes & Williams, 2011).

- Uwe Gensheimer immediately recognizes an opponent's passing feint and can steal the ball.
- Stine Bredal Oftedal scans the defensive behavior of the opposing team and can play into open space based on this.

For example, an athlete has to precisely understand the game situation within a short space of time to be able to react correctly. Interactions with teammates and reactions to opponents are elementary in games, because without exact information from the environment, it is difficult to plan an appropriate course of action (König, 1991). Various aspects of perception are relevant, such as the position of opponents, free spaces, and distances.

Perception is defined as the subjective impression of our environment or our body, shaped by the sensory processing of stimuli from various sensory modalities. Put simply, perception describes the process of receiving, selecting, and processing different stimuli and forms the basis of human knowledge, experience, and action (Marr, 1982). Individually made experiences are based on information which a person receives through senses and processes, and stores in subcortical and cortical recognition structures of the different perception systems (Bruce, Green, & Georgeson, 1996). Perceptual processes therefore initially include all activities that serve to obtain information. Human perception takes place through one or more senses and helps to grasp and classify the environment. Visual perception plays a very important role in many everyday situations, as well as in sport. It describes the absorption and transmission of various stimuli with the help of the eye—in short, the sense of sight. From a physiological perspective, visual perception involves the absorption of photons using photoreceptors in the eye and the conversion of these stimuli into electrical signals, which are first recorded, processed, and interpreted in the occipital area of the brain and then in many other brain regions. On the psychological level, visual perception represents the recording of colour, form/shapes, or movement. These components represent one of the most important ways of perceiving one's environment for humans, as various situations are usually interpreted and decisions made on the basis of visual perception (Memmert, Hüttermann, & Kreitz, 2019).

In the following, various findings, which can be roughly classified into the following four areas, are discussed (see table 2).

Table 2 Classification of the previous findings on perception training in sports

	Information ability of the athlete (intention to act)			
Information processing of the opponent	Conscious	Correct	Conscious	Incorrect (deception)
	Unconscious	Correct	Unconscious	Incorrect (deception)

Conscious Perception Processes Based on Correct Information

Conscious perceptual processes based on correct information have been the most intensively investigated. Most research approaches determine the perception strategies of sports players on the basis of eye movement analyses (for an overview Hüttermann, Noel, & Memmert, 2018; Kredel, Vater, Klostermann, & Hossner, 2017). In summary, it can be shown that experienced players have learned to improve their perceptual performance through targeted strategies (Williams et al. 2010). In an overview article by Mann, Williams, Ward, and Janelle (2007), differences in perception strategies between experts and novices were discussed. The experts used fewer but longer gaze fixations, which are mostly directed at fellow players and opponents (cf. figure 3). Not surprisingly, experts recognized game scenes more accurately than less experienced athletes (North et al., 2011).

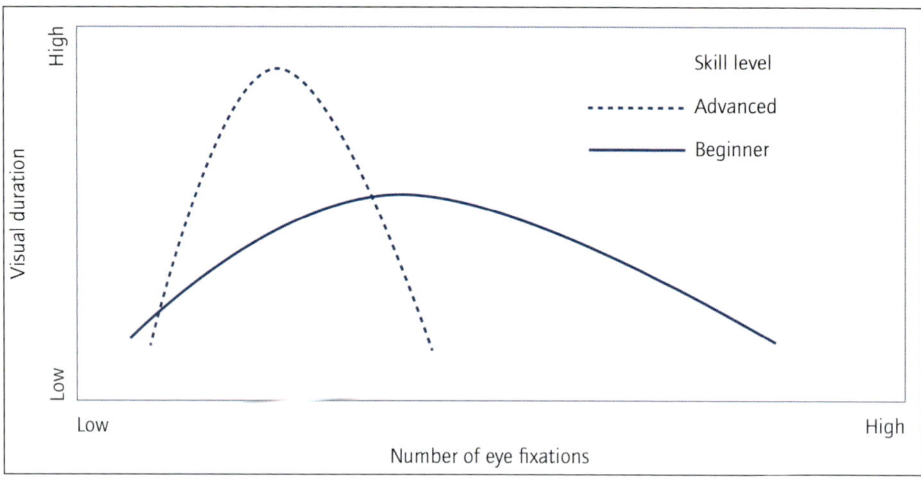

Figure 3 Generalized relationship between number of fixations and duration of fixations (from Tenenbaum, 2003, p. 197).

There are now six studies in handball that have gained insights using eye movement registration (reviewed by Loffing, 2017; critically discussed in Schorer et al., 2018). This shows that excellent handball players can already infer the intention of teammates and opponents before a corresponding action has been performed. They know at which relevant body regions of the opponent and locations on the playing field as well as at which time perceptual information in their environment are particularly important (i.e., information-rich areas; cf. the figure in section 3.1), and they linger longer at these locations with their gaze (a saccade) (cf. figure 3). In this case, fixation has occurred at the center of the critical event (e.g., final phase of the stroke movement from a handball seven-meter throw), so that all relevant information can be processed through foveal and parafoveal processes (cf. Schorer et al., 2018).

Trainers can help the players to select and focus on the right sources of information. These information-rich areas can be dependent on one's own previous knowledge (e.g., knowledge of the opponent) (Jackson, Warren, & Abernethy 2006) and increase perception through greater efficiency. Trainers can unintentionally draw attention to unimportant and somewhat irrelevant aspects of the action by their instructions. For example, the sentence "Do not pay attention to the goalkeeper" has the exact opposite effect on most players; the result is a more extended focus on the goalkeeper and more shots aimed in his direction (Bakker, Oudejans, Binsch, & van der Kamp, 2006).

Conscious Perception Processes on the Basis of Incorrect Information (Deceptions)

A form of consciously used but incorrect perception information is transported by deceptive actions (for an overview, Güldenpenning, Kunde, & Weigelt, 2017): For example, an attacker tries to deceive the defender during a dribble by feinting. Many studies have demonstrated that feints are useful and effective. Not surprisingly, experts in sports games can not only detect a feint at an earlier stage than novices (cf. Sebanz & Shiffrar, 2009), but they are also more likely to predict shots with deception than novices (Bishop et al., 2013; Smeeton & Williams, 2012).

Specifically, handball players also react faster to deceptions that are consistent with the normal direction of the deception maneuver than when this is not the case (Güldenpenning, Machlitt & Schack, 2011). However, it should also be mentioned that in handball there are more studies from the goalkeeper's perspective than from the field players' perspectives (Güldenpenning et al., 2017). An exception is the study by Cañal-Bruland, van der Kamp, and van Kesteren (2010), which showed that while experienced handball players and goalkeepers were superior to novices in detecting deception, no differences were observed between field players and goalkeepers. The authors concluded from these results that neither the level of motor expertise nor the level of perceptual experience per se seems to be responsible for explaining the successful identification of deceptions.

Unconscious Perception Processes Based on Correct Information

Environmental stimuli can be perceived both consciously and unconsciously. Today we know from general psychology and motor research that perception and action influence each other (Prinz, 1997). This could be demonstrated in a series of experiments within the framework of a penalty shoot-out situation (Masters, van der Kamp, & Jackson 2007; Weigelt, Memmert, & Schack, 2012; Noel et al., 2015). The study shows that even unconsciously perceived information can strongly influence motor actions (see box).

Unconscious Perception Influences Conscious Behavior

In numerous studies conducted by working groups from Amsterdam, Paderborn, and Cologne, the goalkeeper's position on the goal line at the penalty kick has been used as a study paradigm to support this statement (Weigelt, Memmert, & Schack, 2012; Noël, van der Kamp, & Memmert, 2015; Noël, van der Kamp, Weigelt, & Memmert, 2015; Noël, van der Kamp, Masters, & Memmert, 2016; Weigelt, Memmert, & Schack, 2012). For this purpose, the goalkeeper was systematically moved slightly more to the left or right of the goal center on the goal line.

In fact, there is a high probability that the shooter will shoot to the right if a goalkeeper is placed to the left of the center of the goal from the shooter's point of view. This effect also exists if the goalkeeper position deviates only very slightly from the center and the shooters do not consciously perceive this shift (Noël, van der Kamp, Weigelt, & Memmert, 2015). Both experienced and inexperienced players are equally influenced by the unnoticeable change in position (Weigelt, Memmert & Schack, 2012).

With the knowledge of this connection, goalkeepers could more consciously choose their position on the penalty kick. By placing the goalkeeper on his weak goal side–minimally away from the goal center–the probability that the shooters aim at the opposite corner increases. This in turn means that the goalkeeper has a higher chance of keeping the shot on his strong goal side.

Unconscious Perception Processes Based on Incorrect Information (Deceptions)

Surprisingly, there are hardly any research studies that address unconscious processes of perception based on incorrect information (deceptions). Güldenpenning and colleagues have argued in their first experiments that false information (i.e., incorrect information) could also be processed unconsciously (Güldenpenning, Steinke, Koester, & Schack, 2013; Güldenpenning, Braun, Machlitt, & Schack, 2015). In this context, skilled handball players seem to use different cognitive processes when processing unconscious stimuli compared to novices (Güldenpenning, Machlitt, & Schack, 2011). This would make it possible for athletes to implicitly process body-related information through priming (i.e., unconsciously perceived information), which in turn can activate motor reactions without being explicitly evaluated.

Studies from the Cologne and Paderborn research groups can also be interpreted as an example of unconscious perceptual processes based on incorrect information, when the goalkeeper shift is made consciously (almost as a deception) by the goalkeeper but is not consciously perceived by the shooter (Noël et al., 2015).

Attention

In the process of evolution the human brain has been optimized to consciously select and process information from the multitude of information that is relevant for goal-oriented action in everyday life, and also in sport (Cohen, Nakayama, Konkle, Stantic, & Alvarez, 2015; Mack & Rock, 1998).

Although attention and perception are closely linked, they are not identical concepts. For example, the spatial distribution of attention differs from the spatial distribution of visual perception (Intriligator & Cavanagh, 2001). Visual perception provides the input for many other cognitive processes, so differences in visual perception can have far-reaching consequences. However, cognition and performance involve much more than the sensory system, and experienced experts can differ from novices in many ways, even if novices have equally good visual perception.

Attention is considered a crucial factor with regard to athletic performance (Abernethy et al., 2007; Memmert, 2009, 2015b; Moran, 1996; Wulf, 2007). Handball players require adequate attentional skills in the simultaneous execution of different activities in order to perform successfully in complex situations (cf. Florkiewicz, Fogtman, Kszak-Krzyżanowska, & Zwierko, 2014; Mohammed & Abdullah, 2018).

For example, in handball, players must guide the ball and shield it from the opponent while simultaneously scanning the game for free teammates. Referees must simultaneously and accurately focus on all relevant information that enables them to decide whether it is a foul or not.

As handball players are continuously confronted with a multitude of visual and auditory stimuli in specific situations of their sports, which they cannot adequately process due to limited processing capacity, the question arises how attention can effectively be directed in order to make optimal decisions. Athletes should be able to direct their attention so that they can select relevant information from the less relevant information. Due to the enormous importance of attention, psychological test methods for measurement have been developed (cf. chapter 4), as well as different models for optimal attention direction in psychology.

The attention mechanism is often explained by the spotlight metaphor: Attention is a type of spotlight whose beam casts light on a specific area (Posner, 1980). The size of the light cone is variable (Eriksen & St. James, 1986) and objects in the center of the funnel can be processed better than information in the periphery (LaBerge, 1983). Since humans have a limited capacity for attention (Broadbent, 1958; Cowan, 1995), they need to hide or attenuate information from our environment in order to work effectively with behavioral events. For this reason, attention theories, paradigms, and mechanisms have already been considered necessary for a long time, and have been intensively studied in cognitive science for almost 100 years (Styles, 2008).

Neuroscientific and cognitive-psychological findings in attention research (e.g., Coull, 1998; Knudsen, 2007; Mirsky, Anthony, Duncan, Ahearn, & Kellam, 1991; Van Zomeren & Brouwer, 1994) suggest a separation of attention into four sub-processes: attention orientation, selective attention, divided attention, and concentration.

Definitions of the Four Sub-Processes of Attention (Memmert & Furley, 2012)

- Attention orientation: Log in and log out the attention for a certain stimulus.
- Selective attention: Select between competing stimuli at a given time.
- Divided attention: Simultaneously distribute attention to different stimuli (multitasking).
- Concentration: Maintain attention to a specific stimulus over a period of time.

Figure 4: Presentation of the four sub-processes of attention based on practical examples (attention orientation, selective attention, divided attention, and concentration) using the example of handball specific requirements (Furley & Memmert, 2009).

Two of the four sub-processes of attention are further described in greater detail below in order to make the attention services relevant in the world of sport (figure 6) as well as more comprehensible and trainable. The focus is on selective and divided attention, because these two play a central role in a lot of sports games. The sub-processes of attention orientation and concentration can be found in detail in a separate section (Memmert, 2009; 2015b).

Selective Attention

The sub-process of selective attention allows a targeted spatial or object-related focus at particular moments in time or within specific periods. While the focus is deliberately on certain events, others are inhibited (i.e., excluded) (Coull, 1998; Posner & Boies, 1971).

Selective attention is closely linked to attention orientation because both of these sub-processes are involved in the direction of attention. However, Posner and Peterson (1990) were able to prove that the two attention processes activate different brain areas (i.e. have different neurophysiological bases).

Selective attention selects from different stimuli, while orientation then logs in attention to this stimulus.

Selective attention is the most considered and discussed component in sports science. This is not only due to the fact that this attention process is the most important in sports-specific situations, but also because there are various ways of methodically examining selective attention. For example, it has been demonstrated that selective attention focus can be manipulated by simple instructions. A small instruction from a trainer can restrict and guide the attention focus in such a way that important circumstances of a situation (e.g., an uncovered player) are not consciously perceived, and thus cannot be included in the decision-making process (Memmert & Furley, 2007). Creative solution finding is therefore severely limited. In a six-month longitudinal study, these findings could be replicated in real training scenarios; children achieved no learning improvement in the creative solution of tactical tasks if their attention focus was permanently restricted by precise instructions and tips (Memmert, 2007).

Divided Attention

In some situations, it is crucial and necessary to selectively focus attention on an object or a place (see section on selective attention). In other situations it is required to process several pieces of information at different places in parallel. The sub-process of shared attention enables athletes to concentrate on two or more sources of information simultaneously (see Coull, 1998). This ability, which also requires a sufficient range of attention focus, is an important factor not only in sports, but also in various everyday situations such as road traffic.

Hüttermann, Memmert, Simons, and Bock (2013) developed a new paradigm with which the visual attention window of a person can be precisely determined. This represents the maximum consciously perceptible field of attention in the horizontal, vertical, and diagonal directions. The attention field is distinguishable from the pure peripheral visual performance. On average, a maximum attention window with a horizontal orientation of 32.88° ± 8.36°, a vertical of 26.40° ± 5.36° and a diagonal of 27.76° ± 5.56° appears. Experts (sports game players) have larger attention windows than novices (non-sports game players), at least in terms of horizontal and diagonal alignment (see figure 5).

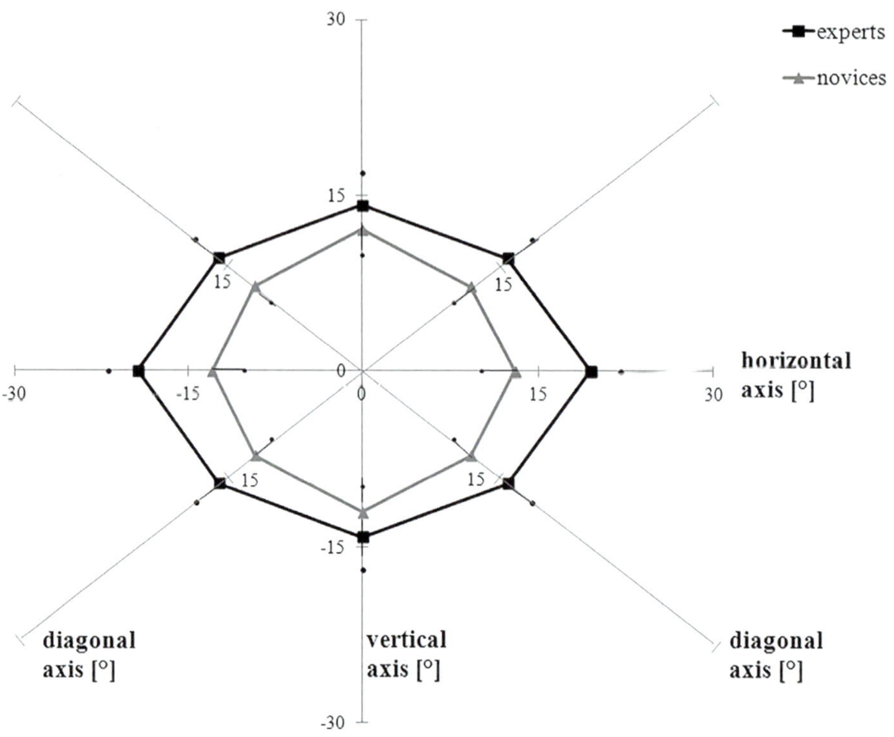

Figure 5 Size of the maximum attention window (in °) for two different athletes from handball during which two stimuli can be perceived peripherally simultaneously. Since each pair of stimuli was presented symmetrically across the center, the data is also presented symmetrically for each axis (horizontal, diagonal, vertical). The external attention window displays the averaged values of a Bundesliga player, the interior window the averaged values of a regional league player, and the error bars indicate the respective standard deviations.

Hüttermann, Memmert, Simons, and Bock (2013) were also able to use the attention window paradigm to clarify the question of whether a fixation between two stimuli is more promising than the fixation of one stimulus with the peripheral perception of the other stimulus. The comparison of both alignment strategies of visual attention showed an average higher success rate (90.42% ± 4.88%) in the identification of simultaneously presented stimuli, compared to the combination of fixed/peripheral alignment (80.24% ± 10.28%). This result seems to be valid for both sports game players and non-sports game players. However, experts in sports games are superior to novices in both strategies.

In the phenomenon of inattentional blindness, the basic idea is that when athletes draw their attention to a particular object, they often do not consciously perceive unexpected objects, even though they are directly and clearly visible to their eyes (Mack & Rock, 1998; Most, Scholl, Clifford, & Simons, 2005).

What Is Inattentional Blindness?

It happens that a player does not see or play towards an utterly free teammate, even though he is clearly in his visual focus. This quickly leads to accusations from coaches and teammates, when the player persistently claims not to have seen his teammate. This player can in fact be right because it is only when attention is directed to a certain area or a particular object that this information is consciously recorded and processed. Conscious perception, therefore, seems to require attention processes. If attention is directed to another object, an unexpected purpose is often not perceived, although it may have been in the visual focus of the athlete.

Even high-level youth handball players have not been able to escape this phenomenon (Furley and Memmert, 2007). If their attention was focused on the direct opponent, they no longer saw the free teammate. Basketball experts in the same situation were also not able to identify free players who would have represented the optimal solution for the game situation (Furley, Memmert, & Heller, 2010). These result patterns were also recognized in more realistic contexts with motor response actions as well as with a task closer to the field (triple choice task) (see figure 6a). Other scenarios which demanded decision-making tasks and complex attention tasks were also able to confirm these findings (see figure 6b).

Figure 6 Illustration of two sports-specific Inattentional blindness test scenarios of different complexity levels (a) low complexity, handball; 3 vs. 3, Memmert & Furley, 2007; (b) medium complexity, basketball, 5 vs. 5, Furley et al., 2010). The free player, who—according to expert opinion—is also the best solution in this situation, is circled.

Game Intelligence

For generating possibilities of decisions and finding optimal solutions, a player must be able to perceive all important information from his environment (teammates, opponents, suddenly appearing players etc.) in order to consider them in his action plan. In handball, the center backs, in particular, have the task of structuring a team's offensive game through smart, rehearsed tactical behavior. In this context, sports science likes to speak of decision-making ability or, based on psychology, of convergent thinking or (game) intelligence.

Definition

tactical play intelligence (convergent tactical thinking)—In team and racket sports, tactical game intelligence means the creation of the best solution to problems in specific individual, group, or team tactical game situations.

Sports games research mainly works with two definitions of cognitive thinking processes, established by the research group around Joy Paul Guilford (1967): convergent and divergent thinking (Roth, 2005). In convergent thinking processes, ideal problem solutions are sought and targeted. Divergent thought processes, on the other hand, generate a multitude of problem solutions, particularly solutions that are new, unexpected, or surprising.

Research on tactical game intelligence is closely linked to cognitive decision research (Höner, 2005; Roth, 2005). In sport, it is often called tactics. At this point, it is not possible to give a comprehensive overview of tactics research in sports games or handball. For this purpose, it is necessary to refer to other works in sports games (Memmert, 2004 a, b; Raab, 2001; Roth, 1989) or handball (cf. Fruchart, Pâques, & Mullet, 2010; König, 1991; König, Greve, & Kromer, 2018; Le Menn, Bossard, Travassos, Duarte, & Kermarrec, 2019; Raab, Zastrow, & Lempertz, 2007; Strykalenko, Shalar, Huzar, Voloshinov, Yuskiv, Silvestrova, & Holenko, 2020; Wagner, et al, 2014; Weigel, 2018). An actual summary of theories and models can be found in König and Memmert (2019).

At this point, the focus is on individual tactical cognitive solutions. This often touches on the construct of (tactical) playing ability (cf. Kuhlmann, 1998; Roth, 2005; see table 3). "The construct of playing ability has undoubtedly become a central guiding idea of game mediation" (König, 1997, p. 209). Thus, the general ability to play sports can be compared with the g-factor in general intelligence research.

Table 3 Definitions of the construct of playing ability in sports games (from Memmert, 2004a, p. 241)

Labelling	Definition	Operationalization	Author
Game intelligence/ tactical flexibility	The ability to find the right decisions quickly in changed, unforeseen situations, and to find solutions in a tactically useful way.	-	Döbler (1964)
Athletic playing activity	Diverse and complex appearance, whose quality is determined by numerous performance factors. From a psychological point of view, it can be seen as a unit of motivational, volitive, emotional, and cognitive processes, which find their manifestation in the sport's game-specific motor function. Characteristic for it is the multiple reference system—player, opponent, ball, target area—in which the player is located and with which he must constantly actively interact.	-	Konzag & Konzag (1980)
General and special playing ability	The ability to initiate a game, back it up as it progresses, and re-establish it in the case of disturbances. The existence of knowledge about the game idea and rules, the necessary skills in handling the game equipment, and tactical experience in important game situations.	-	Dietrich (1984)
Playing activity	Targeted conscious tactical maneuvers. The tactical knowledge is the basis for the perception and analysis of the game situation and for the game performance.	-	Herzog (1986)
Playing ability	The complex ability to solve the various and constantly changing game situations even under opponent interference.	-	Stiehler, Konzag & Döbler (1988)
Tactical action	The appropriate and effective coping of complex game situations.	X	Wegner & Katzenberger (1994)

Playing ability	The ability to participate actively and successfully in a sports game as a teammate and opponent by coping with typical game situations and game processes within the framework of the rules, technically and tactically, individually or in teamwork with others, by experiencing and shaping the game emotionally.	-	König (1997)

As table 3 shows, there are numerous, sometimes even quite different concepts and systematics, as well as contradictory definitions for the construct of playing ability (for detailed discussion see König, 1997, p. 476).

Basic tactics play a significant role in the development of general playing ability or game intelligence (cf. Memmert & König, 2012). They can be described as basic tactical knowledge that plays a central role in many sports games (cf. table 4). In the meantime, they have become an integral part of numerous curricula and training concepts in various age and performance categories (general ball school: Kröger & Roth, 1999; Roth & Kröger, 2011; ball school rebound games: Roth, Kröger & Memmert, 2002; ball school throwing games: Roth, Memmert & Schubert, 2006; ball school in primary schools: Roth, Damm, Pieper & Roth, 2014; soccer: Memmert, Thumfart & Uhing, 2014) and of course in handball (Hohmann & Pietzonka, 2017; Knobloch, Pieper & Uhrmeister, 2020).

Table 4 Basic tactics in handball

• ATTACKING THE GOAL: Tactical tasks in which it is important to select the time and place of a final action.
• MOVING THE BALL TO THE GOAL: Tactical tasks in which it is important to transport the ball into an offensive or goal area.
• INTERPLAY: Tactical tasks in which it is important to pass on the ball to teammates quickly according to the situation.
• USING GAPS: Tactical tasks in which it is important to use (individually) gaps for the chance of playing or winning points when dealing with opponents.
• FEINTING: Tactical tasks in which it is important to ensure (individually) control of the ball and being confronted by opponents.
• CREATING A MAJORITY: Tactical tasks in which it is important to create an advantage by offering and orienting in cooperation with the teammates.

The primary tactics in table 4 can be used as a first starting point for tactical game types, which can help to train tactical game intelligence in club training, in talent development, and in the preparation of beginners in school (educational plans for playing ability).

Example: Testing the Effectiveness of Tactics Training in the Field

As an example, the research program Bilateral Training in Children's Handball (Weyermann & König, 2021) will be used to show how training effects can be evaluated with regard to the specific tactical competence of bridging space cooperatively in handball. One goal of the research program is to investigate the effects of a two-sided handball-specific technique-tactics training on individual tactical attacking behavior in children's handball. Improvements in the quality of technical execution as well as individual tactical performance development can be expected. Bilateral training seems to have the potential to train the perception of non-dominant spaces and thus lead to a broader focus of attention, which in turn facilitates and expands creative performance.

The playing field of the test situation for bridging space cooperatively consists of two halves of the game (2 x 6m x 6m [cf. figure 7]), in each of which there is one defender. Two attackers start with the ball from the starting line; their aim is to bridge the playing field in a situation-appropriate manner and at as high a speed as possible (in order to subsequently execute a goal throw, which is not evaluated). Bouncing, crossing, and passing are allowed. The defenders try to win the ball or to provoke a loss of the ball by skillfully closing the spaces and attacking the attackers; however, they are not allowed to leave their half of the field.

Using a nine-point rating scale, the ball-possessing attacking player is evaluated to what extent the WHAT decision is functional and flexible (VP achieves the situational task goal and shows variable, versatile, original [also ambidextrous] non-stereotypical solutions), the HOW decision is

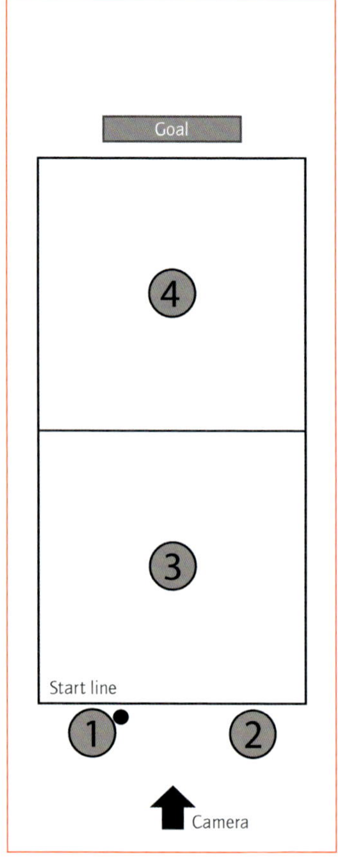

Figure 7 Handball-specific game test situation for bridging space cooperatively (Russ, 2020).

functional (the execution of the movement structure aims at a functional goal achievement), and the timing is situationally appropriate (the timing of movement actions [play-off, running path, goal throw, etc.] is situationally appropriate). The characteristic values range from usually situation-appropriate with flexible solutions (8 points) to situation-appropriate with flexible solutions balanced with situation-inappropriate and stereotypical solutions (4 points) to mostly situation-inappropriate and stereotypical solutions (0 points).

Game Creativity

If you ask handball experts or take a close look at top international handball, you can see that it's the highly creative athletes who can make the difference. For example, Mikkel Hansen was named World Handballer in 2011, 2015, and 2018. Nikola Karabati⍰, who plays with Mikkel at French Champions League club Paris Saint-Germain, has also been named World Handball Player of the Year three times. In the women's category, creative player Cristina Neagu has even won four titles. And "Andy Schmid is capable of variably solving many, sometimes unusual and thus surprising situations" (Dr. Rolf Brack about Andy Schmid, personal communication on 22/03/2021). In addition to tactical game intelligence, another cognitive-thinking process plays a significant role in handball: tactical creativity.

Importance of Creativity in Other Sports

Joachim Löw's statements attest to the special importance of creativity in soccer: "Creativity and playing class should be the new German virtues." The former sports director of Bayern Munich, Matthias Sammer, also points out their importance: "The first initiative to increase flexibility in our own team always came from the coach. [...] Only we felt that our game had to become more creative and unpredictable. [...] Only then was our style of play unpredictable and modern—extremely creative." The former captain of the German national soccer team, Philip Lahm, responds to the question of whether automatisms and a plan can stifle creativity: "The plan is the basis, the game continues to live on creativity and spontaneity in the individual situations. Nevertheless, you basically have to know how you want to defend against a diamond, for example."

Definition

tactical creativity (divergent tactical thinking)—In team and racket sports, tactical creativity is the generation of numerous solutions to problems in specific individual, group, or team tactical game situations that can be described as surprising, rare, and/or original.

Creativity in handball means particularly surprising, original and flexible, tactical and motor solutions such as no-look passes, ground passes, or certain running routes. Empirical evidence on the importance of tactical creativity in handball is still lacking, but in professional soccer there is initial evidence (Kempe & Memmert, 2018).

Is Creativity a Strong Element in Professional Sport?

There is no data at the moment on the importance of tactical creativity for professional team handball. However, a recent study in professional soccer could transfer and contribute to team handball as well. Memmert and Kempe (2018) have examined all matches of the 2010 and 2014 World Cups and the 2016 European Championship in soccer for creative actions in scoring goals. All goals that emerged from the games were analyzed, which equates to 311 goals in 153 games. In each case, the game situations and actions that resulted in a goal were evaluated. The last eight actions that resulted in the goal were included. Three soccer experts with UEFA licenses had the task of rating the actions before the goal, in terms of creative performance, on a scale from 1 to 10 with 1 representing a significantly below-average level of creativity, and 10 a significantly above-average level of creativity. The results show that the level of creativity increases as the actions get closer to the goal. The seventh action, in particular—the decisive pass or assist—received the highest average level of creativity. Overall, the last three actions before the goal shot had significantly higher creativity values than the actions before. Even if these values are only slightly above the average, this shows that highly creative solutions are extremely rare. The experts rated only 172 out of over 1,800 actions as highly creative, with a score of 8 or higher on the creativity scale. On the other hand, in almost half of all goals (46%), the action sequences contained at least one action with a high level of creativity. For the very successful teams of the three tournaments, the figure was even 63%. Memmert and Kempe (2018) were also able to show that creativity distinguishes successful from less successful teams in a tournament. In summary, creativity seems to be an increasingly important factor in soccer, particularly when it comes to scoring goals at the highest level of performance.

In order to be able to evaluate such a broad term as tactical creativity, Guilford's research group operationalized it in 1967, dividing it into three properties: originality, flexibility, and fluidity. In handball, video tests (Furley & Memmert, 2015; Memmert, 2010a, b; Memmert, Hüttermann, & Orliczek, 2013) and game test situations (Memmert, 2004a, b, 2006, 2010b) were developed to operationalize these three factors.

- Originality: The unusual tactical decision actions can be evaluated by handball experts.
- Flexibility: The variety of tactical decision actions is determined by the variety of actions or responses of the handball players.
- Fluidity: The number of tactical decision actions that handball players generate for a particular situation constellation.

In recent years various national and international empirically driven research programs (for an overview: Memmert, 2012; 2015a; also Santos, Memmert, Sampaio, & Leite, 2016; de Sa Fardilha, & Allen, 2019) have developed numerous methodological options for handball-specific training of tactical creativity (Hossein, Mehdi, & Mohammad, 2018; Tanggaard, Laursen, & Szulevicz, 2016). Meanwhile, neuroscience approaches are also increasingly used to better understand the emergence and processes of tactical creativity (Fink et al., 2018, 2019; Rominger et al., 2020, 2021). On a methodical level, the seven principles—the seven Ds of creativity training in handball (deliberate play, one-dimensional games, diversification, deliberate coaching, deliberate memory [discussed in the next chapter], deliberate practice, and deliberate motivation)—seem to be of particular importance (figure 8). Their arrangement is deliberate and corresponds to chronological order.

While the first four principles seem more suitable for child and youth training, all seven principles can also be used in adult training. The Ds can, for example, be taken into account for teaching handball-specific tactical content (e.g., basic tactics: Memmert & Breihofer, 2006; Memmert, Thumfart, & Uhing, 2014), but also basic tactics for all sports (general ball school: Roth & Kröger, 2011; ball school, racket games: Roth, Kröger & Memmert, 2002; ball school throwing games: Roth, Memmert & Schubert, 2006).

Figure 8 The seven Ds of tactical creativity training in handball (Tactical Creativity Approach by Memmert, 2015a).

1 Deliberate Play

Unguided and unrestricted experimentation in play and unstructured situations during childhood is called deliberate play (Côté, Baker, & Abernethy, 2007). Movement biography studies and field experiments indicate that deliberate play in childhood and adolescence has influenced the creativity of current national team players and Bundesliga players. Unaccompanied action can thus lead to a wide variety of responses and also seems to contribute to intrinsic motivation (Kröger & Miethling, 2020).

2 One-Dimensional Games

With one-dimensional games, you can develop a general and handball-specific tactical creativity which can be characterized as follows (Memmert, 2004a, b; Memmert & Roth, 2003):

- Focusing on one basic tactic (not several!)
- Defining clear role distributions in the game
- Defining specific framework situations
- Guarantee of repeating framework situations
- Guarantee of consistent framework situations
- Guarantee of high repetition rates
- Guarantee of different teammates and opponents through systematic rotations

3 Diversification

Tactical creativity can be trained with game overlapping situations, in which children and teenagers solve tactical tasks with hands, feet, and hockey sticks. Dealing with many different sports-specific situations allows them to gain a variety of movement experiences (Memmert, 2006b). For the creation of original solutions, it is essential for children and adolescents to play with various balls at a relatively young age in the movement biography, and to learn to act in different types of games with different motor requirements in order to think about these kinds of situations repeatedly.

4 Deliberate Coaching

A broad focus of attention is necessary to perceive sudden subjects such as free players, who can be the starting point for original solutions (Memmert, 2005). Fewer instructions from the coaches (deliberate memory) can help children and adolescents to generate creative and varied solutions. Young handball players, who are constantly confronted with attention-grabbing instructions in the training sessions, can be distracted through the interruption. To promote tactical creativity it is not advisable for the trainer to continually stop the practice game and give tactical instructions to the players, as these instructions limit the focus of attention (Furley & Memmert, 2007).

6 Deliberate Motivation

Results from social psychology suggest that creative performances can be manipulated by instructions. This can happen, for example, if the type of instruction influences the emotional state of the respondent during the task. Memmert and colleagues (2013) were able to show that tactical creativity in sports benefits from a focus on hope (promotion focus) and decreases with a prevention focus. A promotion focus accounts for regulating pleasure as a positive result of action and suffering as an absence of positive results. A prevention focus, in contrast, refers to the pleasure in absence or successful avoidance of negative events, and suffering is when they occur. Overall, the results indicate that coaches who are using appropriate instructions to promote the focus ("Your goal is to play every third ball into the gap!" instead of "You must play every third ball into the gap!"), support the generation of creative solutions in handball-specific situations. Debanne and Laffaye (2015) were also able to show, based on regulatory fit theory, that relationships exist between players' motivational orientations and their performance on handball penalty throws.

7 Deliberate Practice

In order to effectively improve specific individual performance criteria, the guided acting in exercise-centered and structured situations is called deliberate practice (Côté, Baker, & Abernethy, 2007). Expertise research demonstrates that competitive athletes need more than 10 years of intensive, sport-specific, and high-quality training in order to have a chance at becoming top athletes (Ericsson, Krampe, & Tesch-Römer, 1993; for an opposite position: see Hambrick & Meinz, 2011; Macnamara, Hambrick, & Oswald, 2014). Memmert, Baker, and Bertsch (2010) proved that future highly creative handball players trained much longer in handball than less creative handball players. Thus, deliberate practice seems to be a necessary, but not sufficient, feature, to promote tactical creativity, especially in late childhood and early adolescence.

Working Memory

The pivot of conscious information processing is the working memory, in which a limited amount of information relevant to the current activity can be processed (for an overview, Baddeley, 2007). The capacity and general functioning of the working memory are of particular importance for cognition in sports (for an overview, Furley & Memmert, 2010).

What Is the Working Memory?

For many cognitive tasks, memory is essential in providing objectives, important attention results, information retrieved from long-term memory, and intermediate results of processing, and to coordinate the processing of all this information. Almost all cognitive processes require the temporary, demand-oriented availability of information. Working memory is thus a key system for understanding complex cognitive performance (Engle, 2002).

Definition

working memory–A term used by cognitive psychologists to describe the ability to simultaneously maintain and process targeted information. As the name implies, the concept of working memory reflects at its core, a kind of memory, but it is much more than just a memory, because it is a memory at work and in the service of complex perception. (Conway et al., 2007)

Although the individual capacity of an athlete's working memory does not seem to influence the different performances in sports games (Furley & Memmert, 2015), coaches should avoid sharing too much information in a tactical briefing or discussion, due to the limited capacity of working memory (Cowan, 2001, 2005).

In addition, it should be noted that the working memory is used to a greater extent when learning new skills (tactical, cognitive, and motor) than in later stages of competence (Maxwell, Masters, & Eves, 2003; Schmidt & Wrisberg, 2004; cf. also figure 9). In contrast to novices, experts do not store specific events (e.g., the paths of individual players, tactical constellations) as individual information units, but rather as tactical patterns of player constellations (chunking processes). On the one hand, this facilitates and improves the early anticipation of significant situation constellations (Williams & Ericsson, 2005). On the other hand, the limited capacity of working memory is not as quickly exhausted by experts as by novices. Thus, it can be used to perceive further situation constellations or sophisticated tactical decision-making processes (Williams, Hodges, North, & Barton, 2006).

The general functioning of the working memory (i.e. the fact that information in the working memory is processed, manipulated, and structured at short notice [Conway et al., 2007]) has significant consequences for decision-making training in sports games. Recent studies (Furley & Memmert, 2013) have shown that the activated contents of the working memory direct the attention focus of an athlete by drawing attention to the objects in the field of vision, to which the contents of the working memory refer. It has also been shown that the working memory capacity allows predictions because it allows athletes to focus their attention by masking task-irrelevant stimuli, thus avoiding disruption (Furley & Memmert, 2012). As a result, and particularly for the principle of deliberate memory as one of the seven Ds, in a positive case instructions of the trainer can direct the attention focus of the athletes and thus facilitate tactical and creative decisions. In the negative case, athletes increasingly resort to irrelevant information from the trainer that prevents optimal decisions from being made through unfavorable attention control in the specific situation (Furley, Memmert, & Heller, 2010).

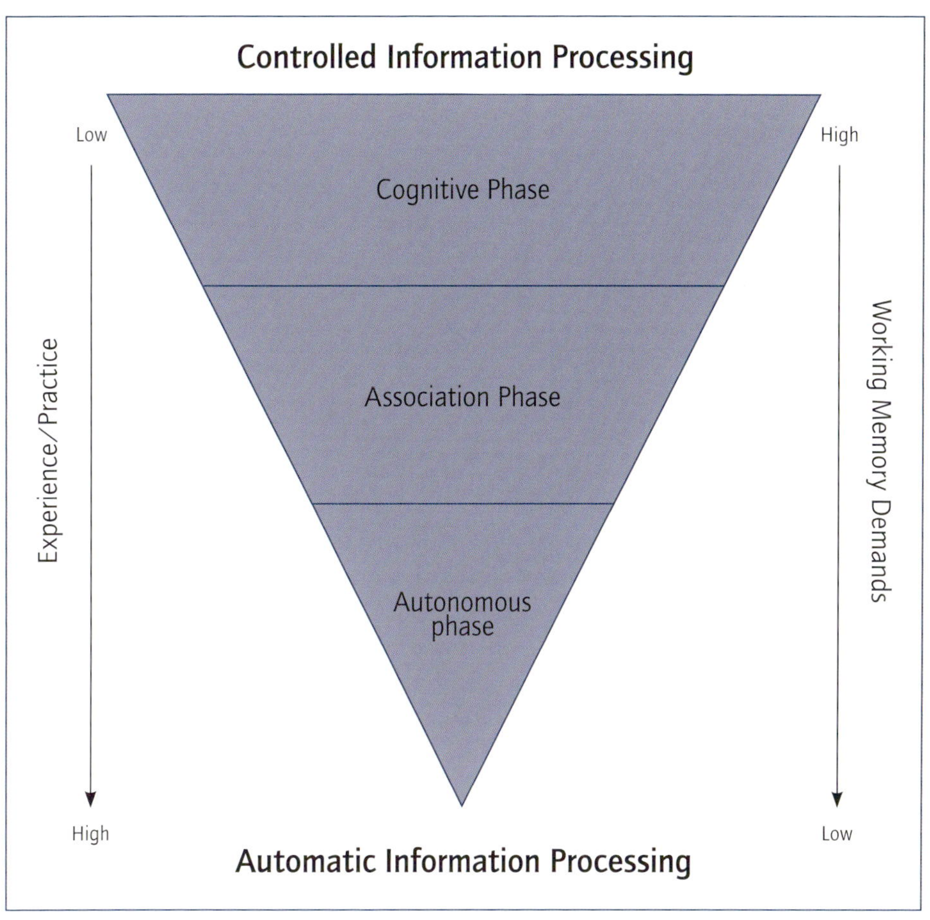

Figure 9 Working memory demands in tactical learning depending on the level of expertise of the athlete (Furley & Memmert, 2010).

4 DIAGNOSTICS OF COGNITIONS

In literature nowadays, an almost unmanageable flood of cognitive tests exists. They range from scientifically proven to pure software products that do not meet scientific criteria. In the following, no general overview is given. However, selected methods which were developed in the last years at the Institute for Training Science and Sports Informatics and were used in studies and the practice are presented. Four laboratory tests and four field tests are also presented as examples.

Laboratory Tests

In the following, four cognitive test procedures are presented. After the testing, the athletes received a summary of their test results compared to different sport-specific test subject groups (see figure 10).

Cognitive Skills

	Attention Window(static)	Working Memory Capacity	Susceptibility to Distraction	Divided Attention (Dynamic)
	The *Attention Window* Task determines the visual field (in degrees) that can be consciously perceived with one gaze, limited by the individual maximum horizontal (h) and vertical (v) orientation.	The ***Working Memory Span Test*** measures an athlete's ability to focus attention on the task at hand without being distracted by other thoughts	The ***Perceptual Load Test*** measures the extent to which athletes, are distracted by external stimuli (plus/minus values = higher/lower distraction), which are completely irrelevant to their task - low (n)/high (h) perceptual load.	The *Motion Option Tracking Test* measures the speed up to which athletes can track multiple, relevant, moving objects.
NN h **NN** v	*	55 %	n -31 h 68	*
Handball h 3. *nat. league* v	16,8 15,2	87 %	n -6 h -3	808
Basketball h *nat. league* v	38,0 36,0	91 %	n 68 h 56	1.251
Soccer h *nat. league* v	40,0 33,0	87 %	n 54 h 33	1.274
Table tennis h *nat. league* v	*	87 %	n -24 h -9	1.204
Handball h *U17* v	15,3 14,3	73 %	n -11 h -10	705
Soccer h *U15* v	24,0 18,0	57 %	n 19 h -8	1.013
Tennis h *U10* v	4,8 5,5	55 %	n 12 h 26	*

Training recommendation:

Test date:

*Not recorded

Figure 10 Presentation of the results of all four elementary cognitions of an exemplary athlete combined with the group mean values of individual other samples (sport discipline, age, expertise).

Attention Window Test

The attention window test (AWT) by Hüttermann, Memmert, Simons, and Bock (2013) can be used to assess the individual's range of attention. During each test phase, players are instructed to fix a central point and try to detect a gray triangle within circle and square distractors. For several attempts, the target will appear at different distances from the attachment point (10, 20, and 30 degrees), along with one of eight equally disputed radial lines from a square in the center of the display (45-degree distance) (see figure 11). This random display is shown for 12 ms, followed by a colored mask (100 ms). After the masking, the players are asked to indicate how many gray triangles they had just seen in the different locations, depending on the orientation of the objects. The participants must complete 180 attempts. This task measures how well people can handle objects far from fixation (Hüttermann, Simons, & Memmert, 2014). The dependent measure is the point distribution of the diagonal attention window and the division of the total value by the number of dimensions (i.e., three).

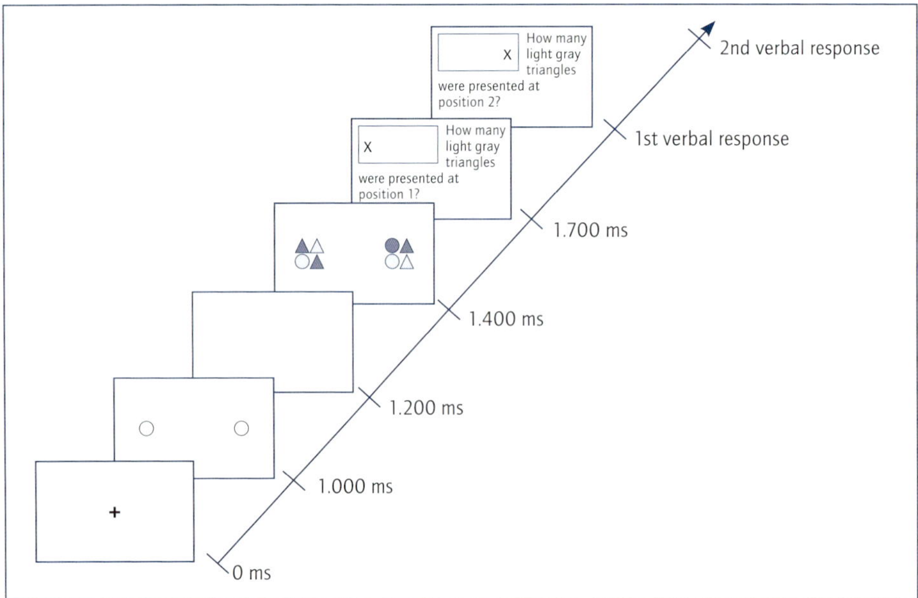

Figure 11 Representation of the attention window test (AWT; Hüttermann et al., 2013). The task is to perceive two stimuli peripherally at the same time. The maximum, still perceptible distance between the stimuli in horizontal, vertical, and diagonal direction is measured and a maximum attention window is determined.

Working Memory Span Test

The established working memory span test of Conway, Kane, Bunting, Hambrick, Wilhelm, and Engle (2005) measures the athlete's ability to draw attention to the task without being distracted by other thoughts. The processing task is to count certain forms between the distractors and then remember the counts for later memory recall. Each task contains randomly arranged dark blue circles, green circles, and dark blue squares (see figure 12). The task is to count out loud the dark blue circles, and then announce the total number of circles at the end. After two to six tasks, a reminder mask appears in which the players have to fill in their memorized totals precisely in the order in which they were displayed (see Kane, Hambrick, Tuholski, Wilhelm, Payne, & Engle 2004, for a detailed description). The simplicity of this counting task permits it to be performed with almost any player. The margin score is a subtotal (see Conway et al. 2005) that represents the sum of all successfully recovered items–where a correctly retrieved item from a set of two items gets 2 points, and a correctly retrieved item from a set of six items gets 6 points–divided by the maximum possible score. The test consists of 15 attempts. The dependent measure is the evaluation of the correctly memorized objects in percent.

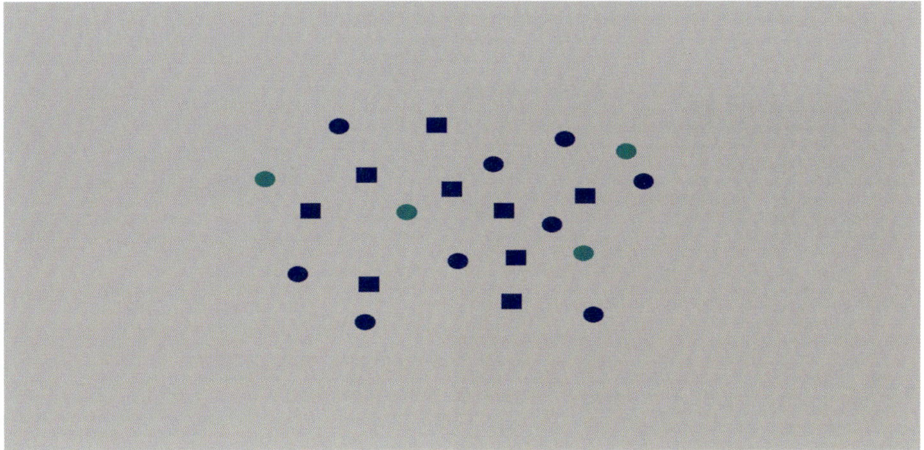

Figure 12 Representation of a display of the working memory span test by Conway et al. (2005). The player has to count out loud all dark blue circles between the distractors (green circles and dark blue squares) and then memorize the totals for a later memory recall.

Perceptual Load Test

The perceptual load test by Beck and Lavie (2005) is a measure of cognitive inhibition since it determines the extent to which players are distracted by stimuli that are entirely irrelevant to their task. The players perform the soccer-specific perceptual load task (Furley, Memmert, & Schmid, 2013) which starts with two example blocks (a high and a low cognitive distraction load); they are followed by eight experimental blocks that alternate between low and high load blocks (figure 13). All players start with one block under high load. Before each measurement, a fixation cross of 1,000 ms is displayed in the middle of the screen, followed by the task display with the soccer-specific arrangement and the distraction maneuver. The task indicators are displayed for 100 ms. Players are instructed to ignore the distraction and indicate as quickly and accurately as possible which player is in possession of the ball. The distraction maneuver is always shown at a fixing point (Beck & Lavie, 2005). The participants react to the target stimuli by pressing a key. A new task is triggered by the player's reaction or omissions within two seconds. After each attempt, feedback on the quality of the answers or omissions is given by means of a computer sound. After each block, the participants are reminded of the critical assignment. The test consists of 160 attempts. The dependent measure is the reaction time of the perceptual stress related to the state of low and high distraction.

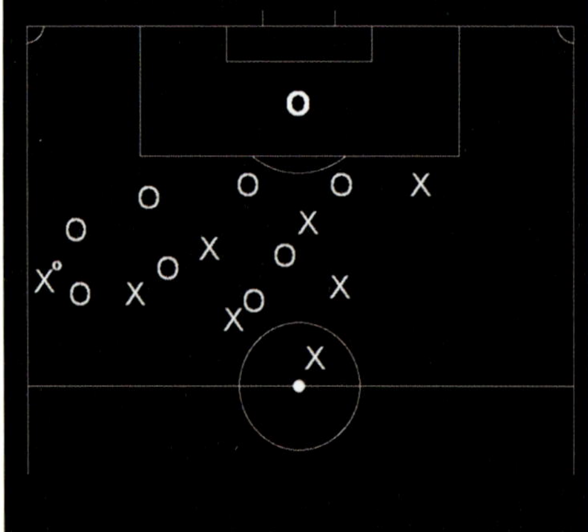

Figure 13 Representation of a display of the soccer-specific perceptual load task by Furley et al. (2013). The players have the task to ignore the distraction (0 in the penalty area) and indicate as fast and as accurately as possible which player is in possession of the ball (0 = defense, X = offense).

Multiple Object Tracking Test

The multiple object tracking test for movement tracking measures the velocity at which players are still able to track multiple relevant moving objects (Alvarez & Franconeri, 2005). 3D multiple object tracking training has positive effects on passing decisions (Romeas, Guldner, & Faubert, 2016), but no significant transfer effects on other visual or executive functions (Scharfen & Memmert, 2021).

The players observe the positions of a series of moving circles on a computer monitor. The display initially contains four green and three blue circles. After three seconds in sleep mode, the blue items turn green and are identical to the targets (green circles), and all circles begin to move as players try to track the positions of the initial green items. The test is adaptable so that the speed thresholds and the number of attempts depend on the abilities of the players. After eight seconds, the circles stop and players must mark the three formerly blue circles. Performance is defined by the number of correctly tracked and marked circles. This task shows individual differences in the ability to divide and maintain attention on several independently moving objects (see figures 14a, 14b, and 14c), but no significant transfer effects on other visual or executive functions.

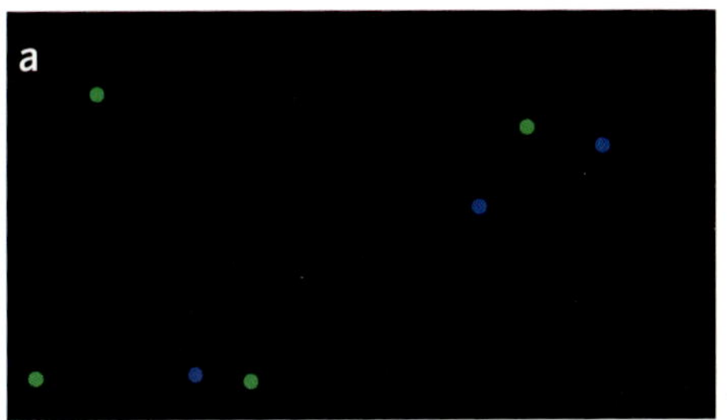

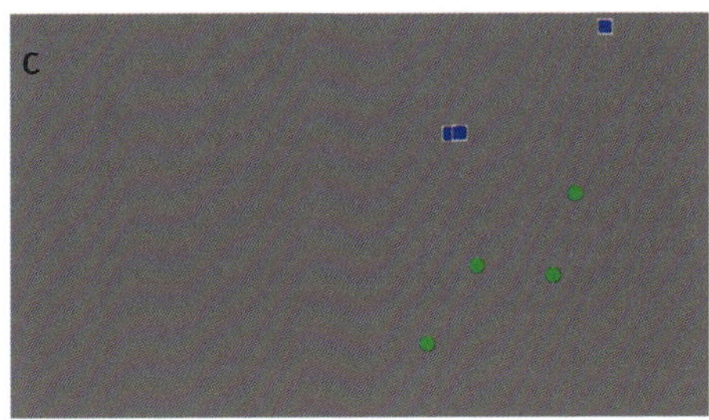

Figure 14 Representation of the Multiple Object Tracking Test (Cavanagh & Alvarez, 2005). The task is to track and recognize several (a) static images for identification, and (b) moving objects at the same time in order to finally identify them at (c) the end of the test.

Field Test

Elementary cognitions are also known as basic tactics in sports games (Memmert, 2004a). Game test situations can make both tactical creativity (Memmert, 2010a, b; Memmert & Roth, 2007) and game intelligence (best solutions) assessable for basic tactical tasks (cf. Memmert, 2010b; Memmert & Roth, 2003; Memmert, 2013). As already described in the chapter on game intelligence, these are basic competencies that are of particular importance in many sports games and form the foundation for later sport-specific (here handball) tactics.

Game test situations can assess both tactical creativity (Memmert, 2010a, b; Memmert & Roth, 2007) and game intelligence (best solutions) in basic tactical tasks (cf. Memmert, 2010b; Memmert & Roth, 2003; Memmert, 2013). The resulting convergent performance indicators can be used for talent diagnostics in clubs or for grading in physical education classes. In the club, it may be useful to use a video camera to record children's behavior and then use a video and scale to assess tactical behavior. At school, the teacher can also use the developed scale to make the assessment directly. As an example, four standardized game test situations with their scales for the evaluation of convergent tactical performance are presented below. They were comprehensively tested with regard to quality criteria of quantitative research (Memmert, 2004a, b). These diagnostic options use the basic module labels from Memmert (2004a). As these are almost identical in content to the basic modules of Roth and Kröger (2011), they are also listed. Game test situations with the scales for evaluating divergent tactical performances can be read in Memmert (2010a, b) as well as in Memmert and Roth (2007).

Game Test Situation: Moving the Ball to the Goal

In this basic tactic (creating a majority), the players should play the ball in the direction of the goal area. For this purpose, it must be assessed whether the player currently in possession of the ball—if it makes sense—has played the ball in a particular direction of the goal area, and if the most considerable possible distance has been bridged (first evaluation criterion).

Furthermore, the decisions of the children should be evaluated under consideration of the situation (second evaluation criterion). From these two components, an overall judgement on the performance of the individual can be derived. In this game test situation, only the player being active on the ball is evaluated; it is not taken into account how well the players offer themselves or orient themselves in a space, and how the interaction takes place (an example from a current research project is shown in the box in section 3.4).

The test situation (cf. figure 15) is performed by the teams A and B playing for the possession of the ball. It is important that the attacking team A is 4:2 in the majority. Team A has to transport the ball over the opponent's finish line. The attacking players are allowed to pass the ball, but are not allowed to run with (follow step rules!), bounce, or carry it. At each attempt, all players of team A are behind the starting line, whereas the players of the defending team B are in the middle of the field. Each attempt begins on a signal from the teacher or trainer once both teams are correctly positioned. The player line-ups of the teams are changed twice counterclockwise after each formation has received six attacks. Thus, each player has 12 attacks with different teammates. The evaluation takes place via an approved scaling (see table 5).

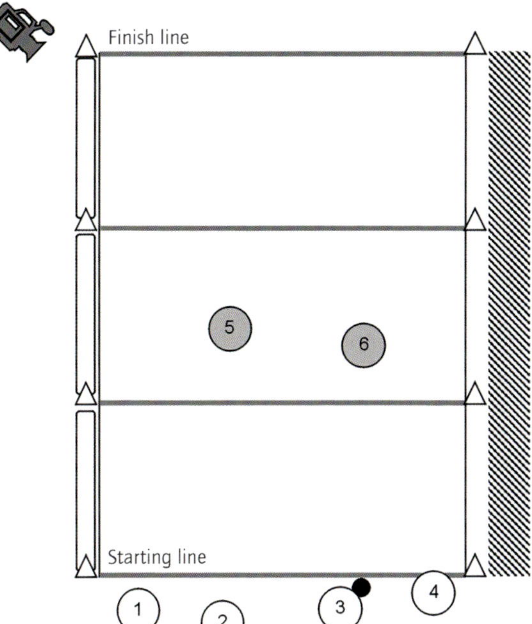

Figure 15 Pitch size = 12 x 8 meters, divided into three equally sized fields; distance between video camera and pitch = 3 meters; starting and finish line.

Table 5 Scaling of the basic tactic: Moving the ball to the goal (Memmert, 2004a).

Play towards the goal area (quality of solution)	Optimal distance minimization	Scaling	Examples
Optimal	Optimal, > 8 m (2 fields)	10	Whenever possible, the player played the ball in the direction of the goal area, bridging as much distance as possible.
Optimal	Optimal, > 4 m (1 field)	9	The player almost always played the ball in the direction of the goal area, bridging a large distance.
Optimal	Optimal, < 4 m (1 field)	8	The player usually played the ball in the direction of the goal area, bridging a large distance.
Good (better alternative exists)	Average, > 2 m	7	The player often played the ball in the direction of the goal area, bridging an average distance.
Good (better alternative exists)	Satisfying, < 2 m	6	The player often played the ball in the direction of the goal area, bridging a satisfactory distance.
Satisfying (better alternative exists	Average, > 2 m	5	The player relatively often played the ball in the direction of the goal area, bridging an average distance.
Satisfying (better alternative exists)	Satisfying, < 2 m	4	The player relatively rarely played the ball in the direction of the goal area, bridging a satisfactory distance.
Insufficient (chose a bad possibility	Average, < 4 m	3	The player rarely played the ball in the direction of the goal area, bridging an average distance.
Insufficient (chose a bad possibility)	Average, >1 to 4 m	2	The player almost never played the ball in the direction of the goal area, bridging an average distance.
Insufficient (chose a bad possibility)	Satisfying, < 1 m	1	The player almost never played the ball in the direction of the goal area, bridging only a satisfactory distance.

Game Test Situation: Interplay

Within the basic tactical game test situation of interplay (cooperative possession of the ball), the ball must be played to a teammate quickly and accordingly to the situation. Two tactical components are evaluated: decision quality and decision time. In decision quality, the spatial decision performance is assessed to determine how well the players can play to free teammates according to the situation. This evaluation takes into account whether the children are taking advantage of opportunities to play a ball in the right moment while under pressure. The second component–decision time–evaluates whether the players are able to find adequate solutions in terms of time, or at which speed a ball is played. Again, only the player active on the ball is evaluated. The result represents an overall assessment of the individual tactical performance in terms of decision quality and decision time.

Figure 16 illustrates the performance with five players. The four attackers stand in the marked fields and are not allowed to leave them. Furthermore, there is a defending player who controls the rest of the field and is not allowed to enter the four squares. The task of the four attackers is to pass a ball as often and as quickly as possible in one minute. Diagonal passes are not allowed so that the player in possession of the ball has a choice out of two pass options. The defending player's task is to hinder the passing of his opponents. After he succeeds, the ball is released again. The attackers are not allowed to play the ball over the defending player using a high pass. After one minute, the positions are changed according to a given rotation direction. Thus, each player has four minutes to attack (see table 6).

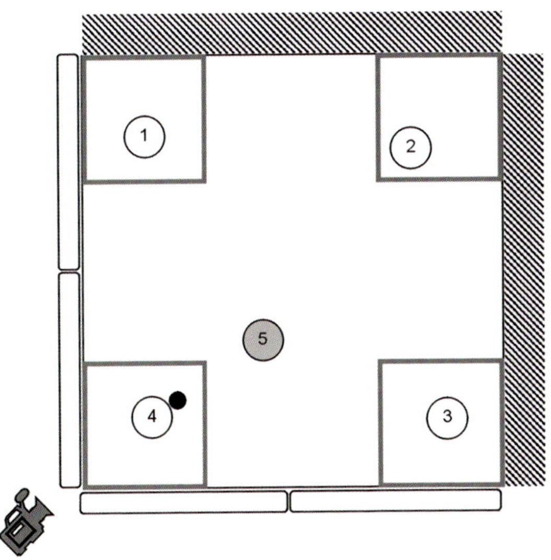

Figure 16 Pitch size = 3.60 x 3.60 meters; side lengths of the four square pitches = 1.0 meters; distance of the video camera (on a mat trolley) to the pitch = 6 meters.

Table 6 Scaling of the basic tactic: Interplay (Memmert, 2004a)

Correctness of decision Adequateness of passing (error/quality)	Decision time/ velocity	Scaling	Examples
Always optimal (no errors)	Slightly delayed	10	Player played up to one critical situation optimally and as fast as possible.
(Few errors)	Never delayed		
Always optimal (no errors)	Slightly/significantly delayed	9	Player played up to 1-2 critical situations optimally, but often with a slight delay.
(Few errors/critical)	Not delayed at all		
Mostly optimal (> 85 %) (few errors/critical)	Significantly delayed	8	Player played the ball with a significant delay and made few errors.
(Wenige Fehler/kritisch)	Gar nicht/leicht verzögert		
Mostly optimal (few errors/critical)	Significantly delayed	7	Player played the ball with a slight delay and made few mainly critical errors.
(Few, mainly critical errors)	Never/slightly delayed		
Mainly good (> 70 %) (few, mainly critical errors)	Significantly delayed	6	Player played the ball as fast as possible and made a couple of partly gross errors.
(Few critical and gross errors)	Never/slightly delayed		
Mainly good (few critical and gross errors)	Significantly delayed	5	Player played the ball with a slight delay and made a couple of gross errors.
(Few, mainly gross errors)	Never/slightly delayed		
Often bad (> 60 %) (several, mainly critical errors)	Significantly delayed	4	Player played the ball with a significant delay and made a couple of gross errors.
(Several critical and gross errors)	Never/slightly delayed		

Often bad (several critical and gross errors)	Significantly delayed	3	Player played the ball with a slight delay and made many critical and gross errors.
(Several, mainly gross errors)	Slightly delayed		
Very often bad (<60 %) (many critical and gross errors)	Significantly delayed	2	Player played the ball with significant delay and made many gross errors. The decision-making was barely recognizable.
(Several, mainly gross errors)	Never/slightly delayed		
Very often bad (<=50 %) (many gross errors)	Independent of the decision time	1	Player played the ball randomly and made many gross errors.

Game Test Situation: Using Gaps

In this basic tactical game test situation (detecting gaps), the players have to identify gaps and then use them appropriately and according to the game situation. It is therefore assessed whether or not the players have recognized the optimal gap. If there is no gap in a particular situation, the players must play in their rows. Again, only the player who is in contact with the ball is evaluated. There is no evaluation of how well the players offer or orient themselves in a space, or how they interact with one another.

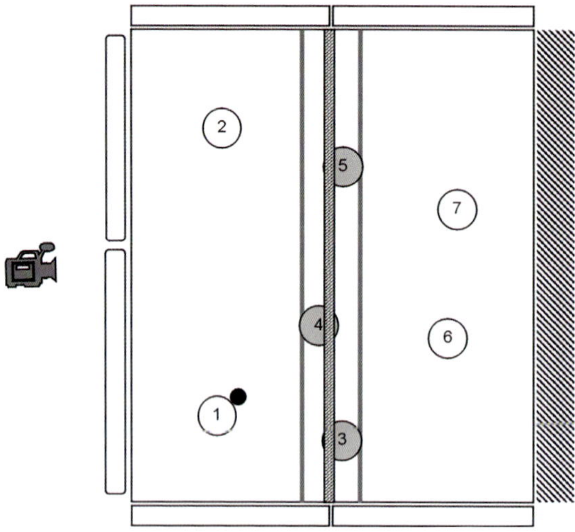

Figure 17 Pitch size = 8 x 7 meters; width of the middle zone = 1 meter; height of the construction site tape above the middle zone = 1.50 meters; distance of the video camera to the pitch = 8 meters.

The attacking team consisting of four players is divided into two players in two attacking zones (figure 17). The defending team consists of three players and acts in the midfield. The defenders are not allowed to leave their zone. Furthermore, the attacking teams are not allowed to enter the defending area. The attacking players have to keep their positions (left or right) and are not allowed to run with the ball. Passing within the two attacking teams is permitted. The defending team always turns towards the player in possession of the ball. After two minutes, the positions are systematically changed so that each player is in an attacking position twice during the game (see table 7).

Table 7 Scaling of the basic tactic: Using gaps (Memmert, 2004a)

Quality of solutions to the situation (using gaps or passing)	Quality of situation	Scaling	Examples
Optimal	Difficult situation	10	Even in difficult situations player made optimal use of the gap or passed to a player with a clearer gap.
Optimal	Moderate situation	9	In moderate situations player made optimal use of the gap except for a few critical decisions.
Optimal	Easy situation	8	In easy situations player almost always made optimal use of the gap and played against a weak defense.
Good, only one better alternative exists	Difficult situation	7	In difficult situations player almost always made optimal use of the gap.

Good, only one better alternative exists	Moderate situation	6	In easy and difficult situations, player made optimal use of the gap except for a few critical decisions.
Satisfying, two better alternatives exist	Moderate situation	5	In moderate situations player made several critical decisions but no serious errors.
Satisfying, two better alternatives exist	Easy situation	4	In easy situations player made some serious errors, but usually recognized the gaps correctly.
Insufficient, bad possibility was chosen	Difficult situation	3	In difficult situations player made several bad decisions, but no serious errors.
Insufficient, bad possibility was chosen	Moderate situation	2	In moderate and easy situations player made many critical decisions.
Insufficient, bad possibility was chosen	Easy situation	1	In easy situations player made several serious errors.

Game Test Situation: Creating a Majority

In this standardized game test situation (offering and orienting), players aim to reach an optimal position on the pitch at the right time (see figure 18). Therefore, the criterion to be evaluated is adequate positioning in the game. Consequently, the players who do not play the ball are evaluated. In contrast to the previous game test situations, this evaluation does not examine whether the player passed successfully, bridged a distance, or orientated toward the goal. Furthermore, the difficulty of the situation is evaluated. The result represents an overall judgment of the individual performance in relation to the positioning in space.

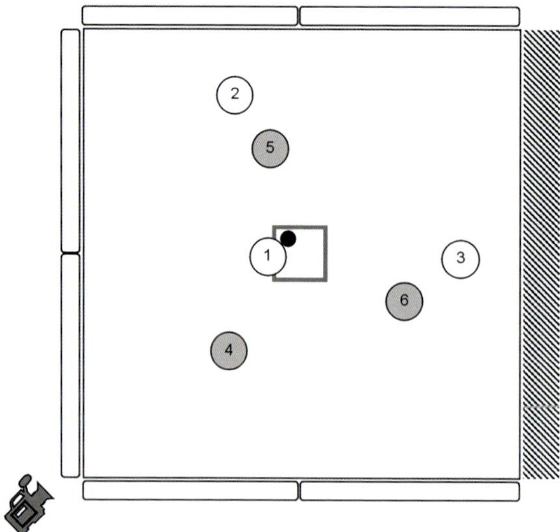

Figure 18 Pitch size = 9 x 9 meters; start square size = 1 x 1 meter; distance of video camera to pitch = 4 meters.

For the game test situation offering and orienting, an attacking Team A and a defending Team B play against each other, each consisting of three players. The task of the attacking team A is to pass the ball as often as possible and not run with the ball. Team B tries to block the passing of the ball. The defending players must keep a distance of two meters from the ball carrier. At the beginning of the game or after an intercepted ball from a defender, an attacker with a ball must be in a predefined starting square. The remaining players can freely move around the pitch. Every two minutes, the players from the three teams are systematically rotated so that each player is attacking twice with different partners during the game test (see table 8).

Table 8 Scaling of the basic tactic: Offering & orienting (Memmert, 2004a)

Quality of performance (adequate positioning in space)	Quality of situation	Points	Examples
Optimal, always available	Rather difficult	10	The player always chose the optimal position in a rather difficult situation and thus always gave the player in possession of the ball the opportunity to pass to him.
Optimal, always available	Rather easy	9	The player always chose the optimal position in a rather easy situation and thus always gave the player in possession of the ball the opportunity to pass to him.
Almost optimal, almost always available	Rather difficult	8	The player almost always chose the optimal position in a rather difficult situation and thus mostly gave the player in possession of the ball the opportunity to pass to him.

Almost optimal, almost always available	Rather easy	7	The player almost always chose the optimal position in a rather difficult easy situation and thus mostly gave the player in possession of the ball the opportunity to pass to him.
Good, frequently available	Rather difficult	6	The player frequently chose the optimal position in a rather difficult situation and thus mostly gave the player in possession of the ball the opportunity to pass to him.
Satisfying, irregularly available	Rather easy	5	The player irregularly chose the optimal position in a less difficult situation and thus sometimes gave the player in possession of the ball the opportunity to pass to him.
Inadequate, almost never available	Rather difficult	4	The player almost never chose the optimal position in a rather difficult situation and thus rarely gave the player in possession of the ball the opportunity to pass to him.
Inadequate, almost never available	Rather easy	3	The player almost never chose the optimal position in a rather easy situation and thus rarely gave the player in possession of the ball the opportunity to pass to him.
Insufficient, never available	Rather difficult	2	The player never chose the optimal position in a rather difficult situation and thus never gave the player in possession of the ball the opportunity to pass to him.
Insufficient, never available	Rather easy	1	The player never chose the optimal position in a rather easy situation and thus never gave the player in possession of the ball the opportunity to pass to him.

5 GAMES FOR COGNITIVE TRAINING

Cognitive training is age-independent (i.e., just as important and necessary for a six-year-old as it is for a Bundesliga professional). Even at an advanced age, cognition can be trained profitably (for an overview: Lampit, Hallock & Valenzuela, 2014; Kelly, Loughrey, Lawlor, Robertson, Walsh & Brennan, 2014; Toril, Reales & Ballesteros, 2014; Shao, Mang, Li, Wang, Deng & Xu, 2015). Elementary cognition and basic tactics across sports games, such as offering and orienting or exploiting gaps, need to be trained very early in beginner and child training.

Nevertheless, if a coach in the district class trains the speed and technique of his players because he wants to work on spryness or passing quality, then he should also train cognition to exactly the same extent if he believes that his team chooses many poor solutions on the field; handball-specific cognition training is not only independent of age, but also independent of playing class. Thus, cognition can be considered as important as speed, strength, endurance, or technique. Handball-specific cognition training is ultimately an important foundation for optimal technique-tactics training. This can be trained in a structured way in all age groups and at all levels of play. For this reason, cognition training should also be anchored more strongly and quite systematically in coach training.

With a view to training control and periodization, solving game situations can find its place in every phase of the season (i.e., in every training session), both in preparation and during the playing season. Handball-specific cognition training can often be integrated very effectively into special forms of games and exercises. Although there are no systematic studies on this yet, one can assume an analogy to technique training (Augste, 2006; Olivier, 1996)—that it might not play a significant role whether cognition is practiced within a unit at the beginning or at the end. The correlation between physical and skill training was overestimated in the past, but this is no longer tenable today.

Players learn just as much when they are rested as they do during or after exertion. In competition, players ultimately have to make good decisions even in the last 10 minutes of a match. Consequently, this situation must be familiar from training. Of course, handball-specific cognitions are also trained casually. In essence, it is about addressing individual cognitions in a targeted and differentiated way to make individual players and the team better. Simply offering game forms and hoping that cognition in handball will be trained as a side effect is unsystematic and falls short.

The following chapters describe a variety of game, competition, and supplementary exercise forms that can train the individual cognitions in handball-specific situations. In doing so, not all the tasks have been reinvented. On the one hand, interesting games were collected from the literature and modified accordingly where necessary. On the other hand, new games were developed and tested in practice. Naturally, not all cognitions have the same number of game forms. While anticipation can be trained extremely specifically, attention can be trained in many different ways. For creativity training, methodological hints are given that coaches can consider in their specific tactical game forms. The descriptions or sketches of the game forms are based on the usual position designations and abbreviations in the specialist literature. They are shown and explained again in figure 19.

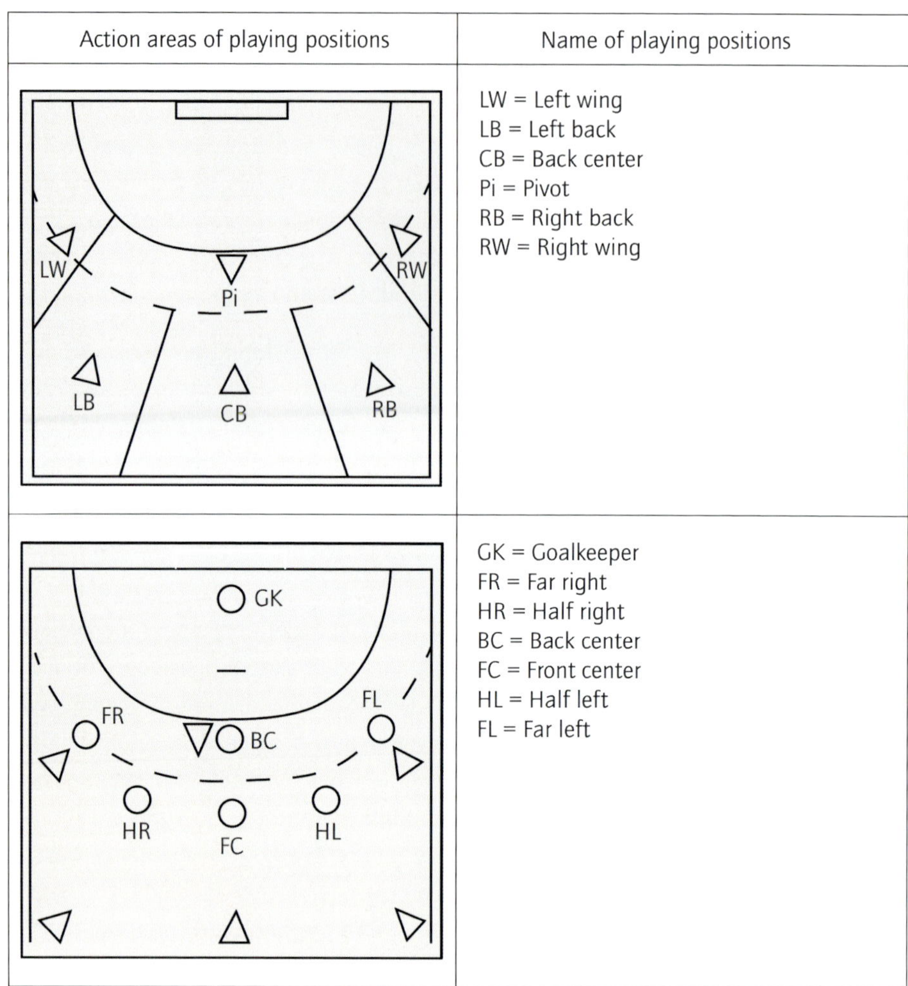

Figure 19 Attack and defense positions in handball.

Basic equipment is needed for almost all exercises. For most forms of play, field markings, several balls, and party bands or different colored shirts are sufficient. If additional materials are needed, such as small boxes, mini goals, other balls, or fitlights, this will be pointed out in the exercise organization. Stopwatches, a set of cards, or whistles can be useful aids to keep times, give signals, and call the group together.

5.1 Games for Anticipation

5.1.1 1 vs. 1 on Half Field

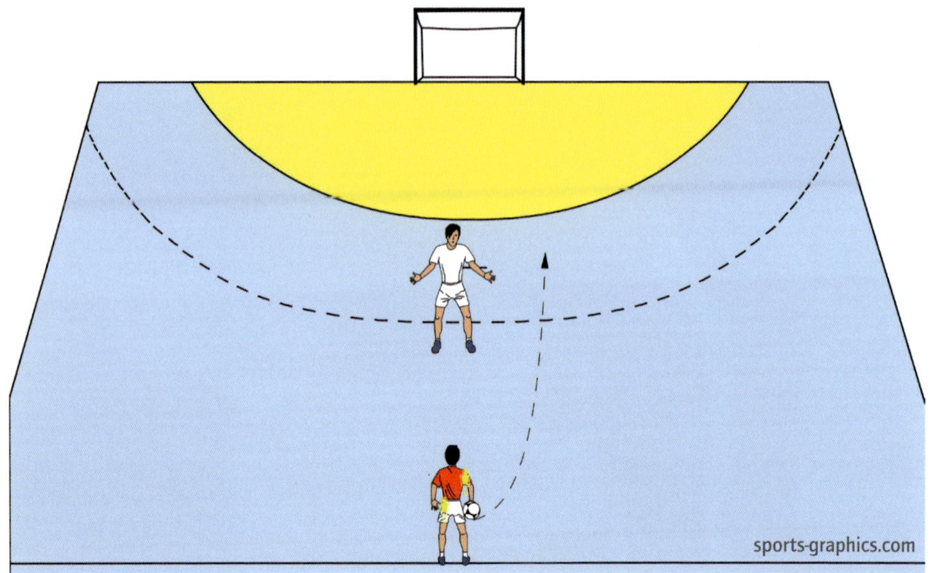

Organization

Two players face each other. The player with the ball (facing the goal, basic position at the center line) has his shoulder and hip marked with yellow sticky dots. The player without the ball or markings faces his opponent at a distance of approximately 2 meters and with his back to the goal. Station 3-4 pairs of players on each half field, starting from different positions.

Procedure

The goal of the attacker is to finish with a goal throw. He begins with restrained speed and opens the action on a signal from the goalkeeper. The defender tries to play the ball out to the attacker while bouncing or pushing him out of the sector. In doing so, he must watch not only the ball, but also the attacker's hip and shoulder. After completing a pass, the two reverse positions.

As soon as one pair has finished, the next pair begins.

Variations

- **Game 1 vs. 1 + 2:** Add two neutral players (one on each side) standing about 11 meters in front of them; first they are static, but later they can start moving. The attacker can run free without the ball after having passed the ball to one of the two neutral players (position LB and RB). The defender mainly watches the hip of the opponent.
- **Second attempt:** If the defender wins the duel, the attacker immediately gets a second ball and starts over again. Deposit the ball box at the center line.

5.1.2 Conquering the Ball in the Game: 5 vs. 3

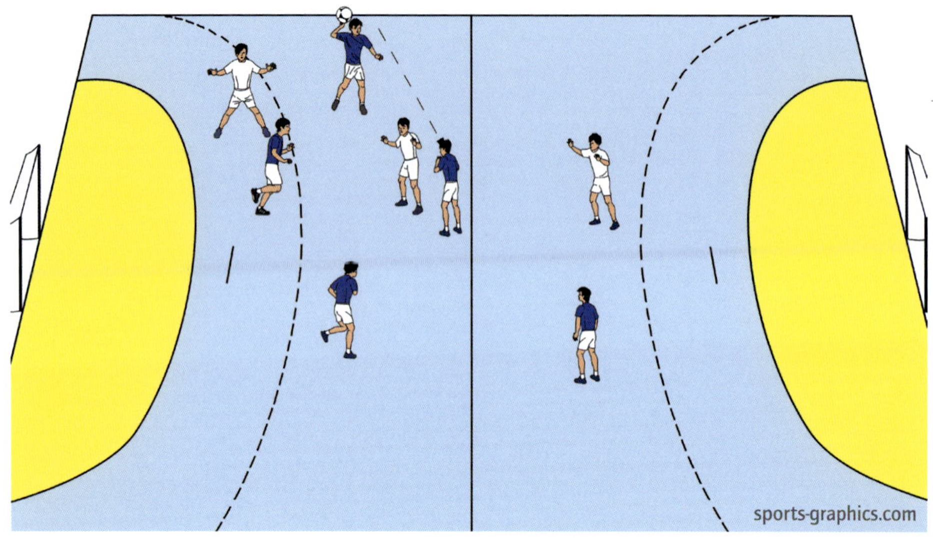

Organization

Five attackers (one ball) play against three defenders. The goal of the defenders is to touch the ball owner. The attackers try to keep the ball in their own ranks for a given time (e.g., 20 seconds) without being touched by an opponent (party ball principle).

Procedure

On a start signal, the five attackers pass the ball to each other. The defenders try to anticipate the path of the ball and get to the ball owner in time. For this, it is necessary that they closely follow the eye behavior and upper body actions of the attackers. If the ball owner is touched, the game starts over again. The goal is to touch the ball owner as often as possible in the given time frame.

Variations

- Depending on the skills and size of the team, other constellations (e.g., 4:2, 5:3 + 1) are possible.
- Change of attack and defense: The defending team has two substitutes outside the field. As soon as someone manages to touch the ball owner, all defenders (3 + 2) become attackers, and three of the attackers become defenders, while two players leave the field.

5.1.3 Wall Ball

Organization

Two teams (team size depends on the number of players and the size of the field) play against each other in one-third of the hall or two or three fields lying crosswise or lengthwise in a third of the hall. The two transverse sides of the field (hall walls) are the goals.

Procedure

A point (goal) can be scored by a player playing the ball as a bouncer against the wall and the bouncing ball subsequently touching the floor. If a defender catches the returning ball, it is not a point (goal).

Further rules: The game is played without bouncing or tapping; a maximum of three steps may be taken with the ball.

Variations

- A point can only be scored when all attackers are in their own attacking half (set center line).
- A point counts double if not all defenders have run back into the defensive half until the ball touches the wall (high tempo of play).
- Combine both variations.
- A bouncer may only be played from a certain line (e.g., from the center line).

5.1.4 Cone Goal Ball

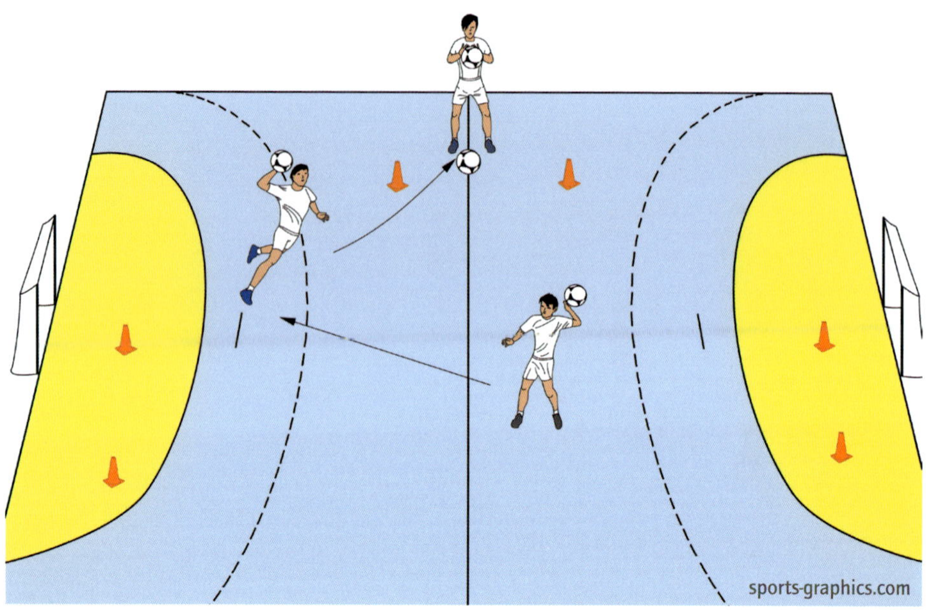

Organization

Two teams play party ball against each other on a field. The aim is to score a point by passing indirectly through one of the three cone goals (all kinds of markings possible) to a teammate.

Procedure

Face-off by draw or jump. The team in possession of the ball tries to position itself in such a way that a ground pass through one of the three goals is possible. The player who catches the indirect pass immediately puts the ball on the ground. From there, the other team continues the game.

Variations

- The successful team continues playing (i.e., scores several points in a row), and the defending team has to win the ball.
- The player receiving the indirect pass has to do so while jumping (both legs in the air).
- The goals can be locked if a defender stands between the marks. Note: More goals than defenders are necessary.

Note

- Depending on the size of the team, set up additional cone goals.

5.1.5 Handball Rugby

The aim of the game is to put the ball behind the opponent's baseline. From there, the defending team starts the game again. **Face-off rule:** foot on the line.

Procedure

The game is opened by a kick-off, jump, or throw-in. Both teams play according to handball rules. Free running is used to get a player into a position to place the ball behind the opponent's baseline without making a step mistake. Rule: The game is played without bouncing.

Variations

- If the player with the ball is touched by a defender, the team in possession loses the ball.
- The point can only be scored by the Kempa element (i.e., receiving the ball in the air and landing behind the baseline; see 5.2.5).
- Ball placement is only possible in marked zones of the baseline (marked by foam cubes, floor markers, etc.).
- The attacking team has to put the ball down behind the baseline after a set number of passes (e.g., 6).

5.1.6 Corridor Handball

Organization

In extension of the goalposts, cones or floor markers are placed from the free-throw line to the center line. These should serve as a boundary between the running path of the attackers and the defensive zone. The width of the corridor can be set at any suitable distance (e.g., 3m, 4m); the decisive factor is the performance level of the players.

Procedure

Two defenders line up in the corridor an equal distance behind each other. One goalkeeper is in the goal if necessary, two goalkeepers alternate at shorter intervals. Two attacking players (A and B, form several groups) line up with the ball at the center line and have to transport the ball towards the goal by skillful passing and bouncing without coming out of the boundary. The defenders try to provoke mistakes and knock out or catch balls. In front of the 6m line a goal is scored by a slap shot. Whoever scores more goals wins.

Variations

- The ball must be transported without bouncing.
- Finish with a jump shot.
- After a team of two completes several passes in a row (i.e., a goal throw), they run back and start with a new ball.

5.1.7 Push-Up Handball

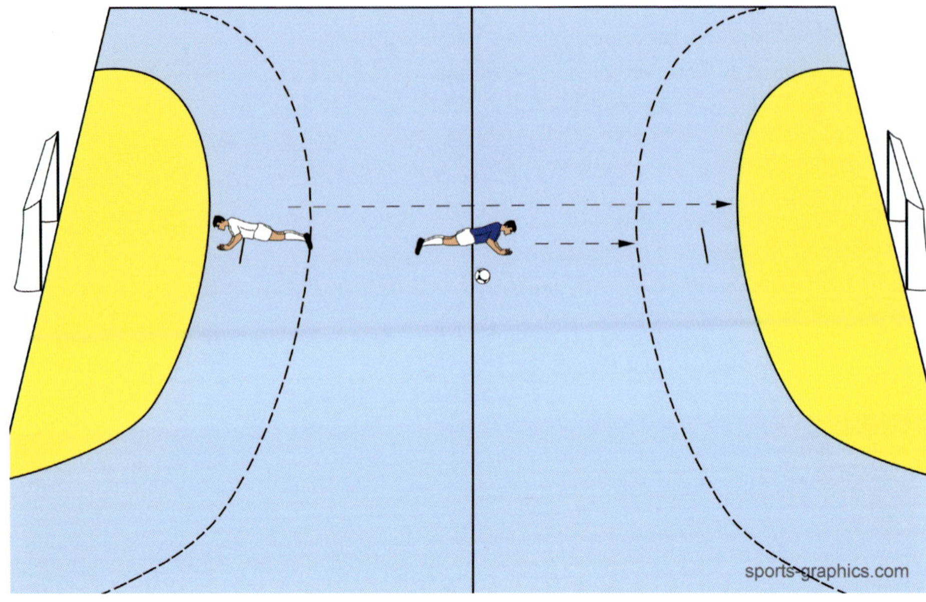

Organization

The players pair up and take the push-up position. A is at the center line, B is at the free-throw line. A is facing the opponent's goal; B has his back to the opponent's goal. The ball is next to A.

Procedure

At the coach's whistle, both sprint to the opponent's goal, A with the ball (Bouncing! Step rule!) and B without the ball. B attempts to reach the goal before A to prevent A from scoring. A tries to score a goal. The players alternate between the positions.

Variations

- The starting position can be varied: Skipping, lying on the belly or back, etc.
- A and B are in the center circle in the push-up position. They try to push the opponent over by pulling their arms away without falling over themselves. It is forbidden to leave the center circle. After a few seconds, the coach throws a ball towards the goal. As soon as this action has taken place, the two players sprint to the ball. The one who has the ball first becomes the attacker, the other one defends. The player who scored a goal gets a point.

- The ball can be put on the floor by the coach or thrown in different directions.
- **Variations of the requirement in the center circle might include:**
  - Clapping their hands on their own lower legs while standing up
  - Pulling out a shirt that has been tucked into the back of their shorts.

5.1.8 Rebounder Ball

Organization

Two teams play against each other on a basketball court (e.g., cross-court in one-third of the hall). Points can be scored by throwing the ball at the basketball board and having it bounce back so that it touches the floor.

Procedure

Player open with a face-off, throw-in, or jump. The team in possession of the ball (A) passes the ball to each other and tries to throw it against the board. Team B has to defend and rebound.

Variations

- A second attacker or the thrower has to catch the rebounding ball.
- Play with double rebound (i.e., the first rebound is caught in a jump and immediately thrown against the board again, the second rebound must touch the floor).
- If a defender touches the player with the ball, the possession changes.

5.1.9 Fast Break 1 vs. 0

Organization

Goal after a given attacking tactical task in a group of two (e.g., crossing or pushing and backing pass or double pushing). One defender stands on the outside position and anticipates the goal throw. Goalkeeper A is in the goal. A ball box is placed next to the goal in order to always have balls ready for the counterattack.

Procedure

LB and RB play push and back pass, LB throws with a jump shot at the goal. The defender (he only has an observation task) does not wait until the ball is on its way (reaction), but anticipates the point of no return (start of the throwing movement); then he starts to counterattack. The goalkeeper deflects the ball and plays a counterattack.

Variations

- Attack tactical tasks vary.
- Both outside defenders act alternately.
- Both outside defenders start at the same time; an extra pass has to be played in the other half.
- If a goal throw is successful, a fast break is played through a fast center.

5.1.10 Fast Break 2 vs. 1

Organization

A and B play a push and a back pass, and are disturbed by an inside defender (2 vs. 1 situation). A throws at the goal. The two defenders (FL/FR) anticipate the situation (without active defensive function) and start the counterattack.

Procedure

LB and RB play push and back pass, LB throws with a jump shot at the goal. The goalkeeper deflects the ball and plays a fast break. Both outside defenders do not wait until the ball is on its way (reaction) but anticipate the point of no return (start of the throwing movement); then both start the counterattack simultaneously. The non-thrower (e.g., B) sprints back and tries to disrupt the counterattack. The counterattack solves the 2 against 1 situation.

Variations

- Attack tactical tasks vary.
- Position an additional defender in the second half.
- If a goal throw is successful, a fast break is played through a fast center.

5.1.11 Fast Break 1 vs. 1 and 2 vs. 2

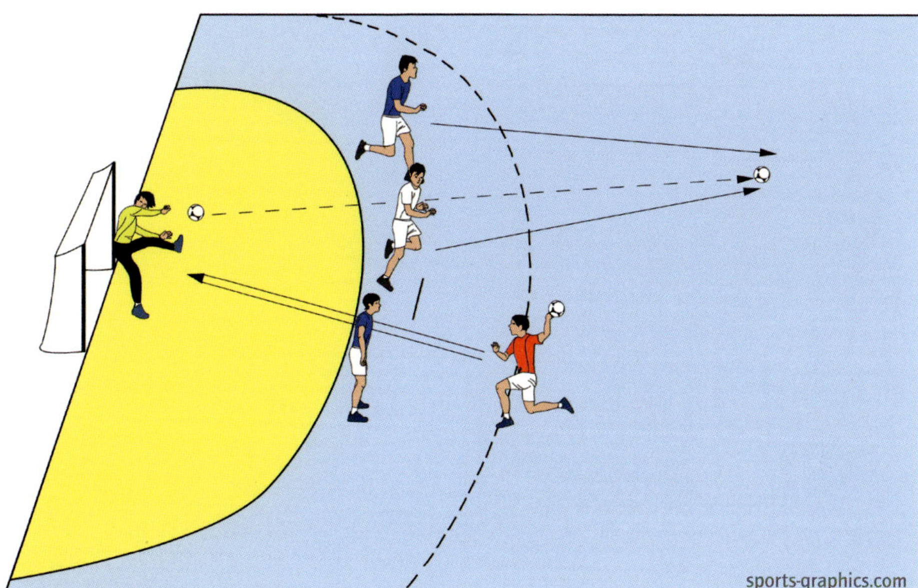

Organization

A and B play a push and a back pass, and are disturbed by an inside defender (2 vs. 1 situation; see 5.1.10); A throws at the goal. An outside defender (FL or FR) observes the procedure (see 5.1.10); the same applies to a neutral player N, who is at the 7m line (in white).

Procedure

LB and RB play push and back pass, A throws with a jump shot at the goal. The goalkeeper deflects the ball and has to play a counterattack. The outside defender and the neutral player N do not wait until the ball is thrown (reaction) but anticipate the point of no return (start of the throwing movement); then both start at the same time. The outside defender runs a counterattack, the neutral player N tries to stop this counterattack.

Variations

- Fast break on both sides in alternation (i.e., occupy the positions FL and FR and two N).
- Both outside backs start and play together. There is one player N running back.
- The non-thrower (LB or RB) additionally sprints back and tries to disrupt the counter-push. The counter-pusher solves the 2 vs. 2 situation.

5.1.12 Variable Fast Break Play

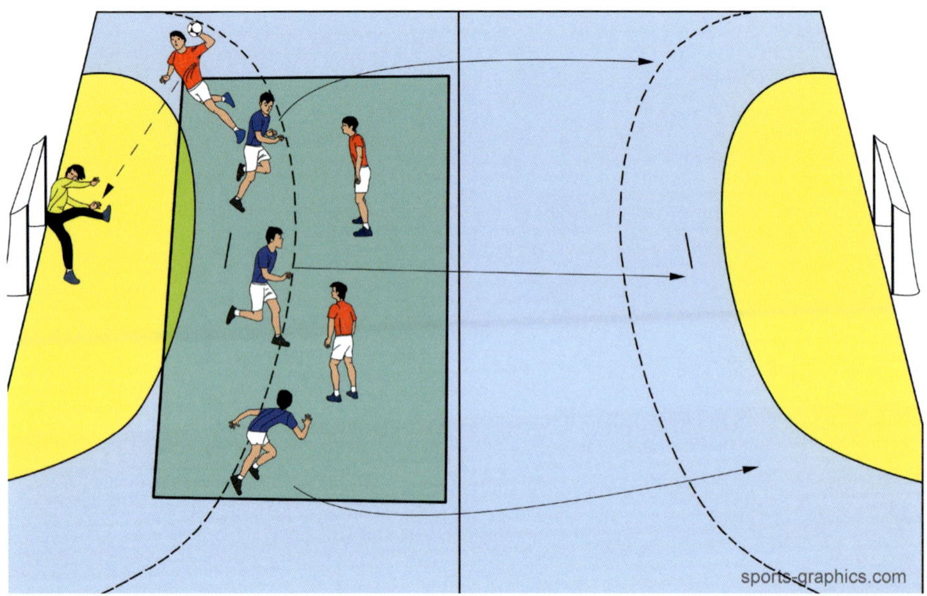

Organization

Two teams of three players play party ball in a rectangle between the throwing circle and the center line. The aim is a lightning-quick switchover of the defense after the attackers have lost the ball or scored at the goal.

Procedure

Team A plays party ball in the marked rectangle against B. Team A, in possession of the ball, has three options:

- Goal throw
- Pass to the goalkeeper
- Put the ball down (in the field)

In each of these three cases, team B must immediately play a counterattack; this also applies if they win the ball. In this case, watch out for signals from the attackers that indicate a certain action (e.g., pass to the goalkeeper). The players of A run back.

Variations

- Variation in team size.
- Variation of the size of the playing field.
- Overscore: The player giving the ball does not run back.
- A rectangle is marked on both sides; counterattack play is alternated in both directions.

5.1.13 Passzeck (Duell, 1981)

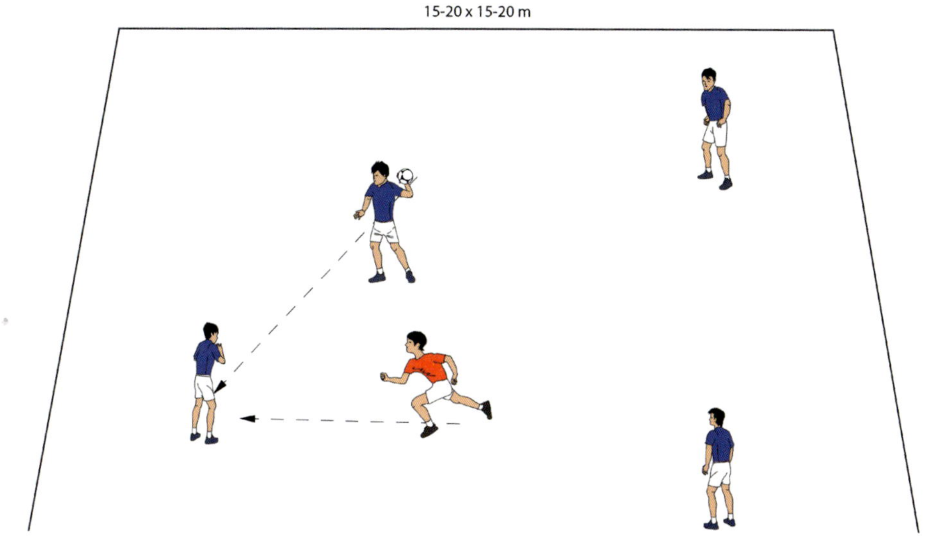

Organization

All players move in a rectangle of 15-20 x 15-20 meters. One player acts as a catcher (be sure to mark him/her in color).

Procedure

The players pass a ball to each other in open running and passing lanes. The catcher attempts to catch an attacker who is currently in possession of the ball. If this is successful, the catcher and the captive alternate the task. A catcher must anticipate possible passing routes in this game; only then does he have a real chance for success.

Variations

- It is played with two balls.
- It is played with two or more catchers.
- Change takes place only after a specified time; the catcher then has to score as many points as possible.
- An intercepted ball results in two points.

5.1.14 Anticipatory Defense (Brack & Bauer, 2020)

Organization

Two cones on the goal area line delimit the left and right action area. One player of each team occupies the left and right pivot position; the action area of the pivots is strongly limited by two marker patches (approximately 1m apart) on the goal area line. One attacker occupies the LW position and one the RW position. FR and HR are positioned in the left action area, while FL and HL act as defenders in the right action area. The remaining players are equally distributed between the LB and RB positions (each with ball); LB1 or RB1 position themselves about one meter outside the free-throw area.

Procedure

HR steps out against LB1 and touches him briefly with his hand. LB1 must then immediately perform a finishing action. He can throw at the goal himself, pass the ball to the pivot, or pass to LW.

HR and FR try to prevent a successful completion of the attackers or make it more difficult by proactively blocking passing lanes.

Then the same procedure follows in the right-hand action area.

Variations

- Opening pass LB/RB with additional CB.
- After the LB/RB pass to CB, LB turns 180 degrees (facing the center line). On CB's signal, LB performs a turn jump (always keeping CB in view!), receives CB's pass in the jump, and then acts as in the basic sequence.
- LB1 has no ball and stands so that he can see LB2. As soon as LB2 passes the ball to him on the floor, LB1 performs a 180-degree turn, receives the ball, and then acts as in the basic sequence.

5.2 Games for Perception

5.2.1 Pursuit Bounce

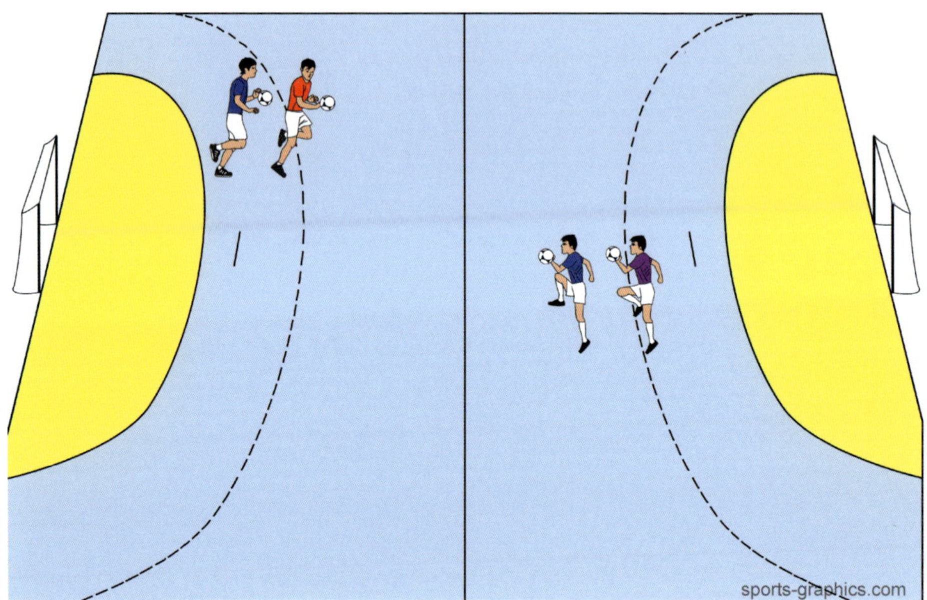

Organization

The players are divided into teams of two. Each player has one ball.

Procedure

In each team of two, player A runs ahead and varies his running movements. Player B acts as a shadow (i.e., he imitates A as closely as possible). Change tasks on visual signal from the coach (e.g., hold up hand, drop marking shirt, sit down).

Variations

- Change of assignment when two players running ahead pass each other closely (i.e., B1 now follows A2 and vice versa).
- The teams of two try again and again to pass between another team of two. If this succeeds, the two shadows change.
- Perform an additional task (e.g., high-five, exchange ball, etc.) before changing assignments (i.e., the time pressure is increased).

5.2.2 Climate Quadrangle

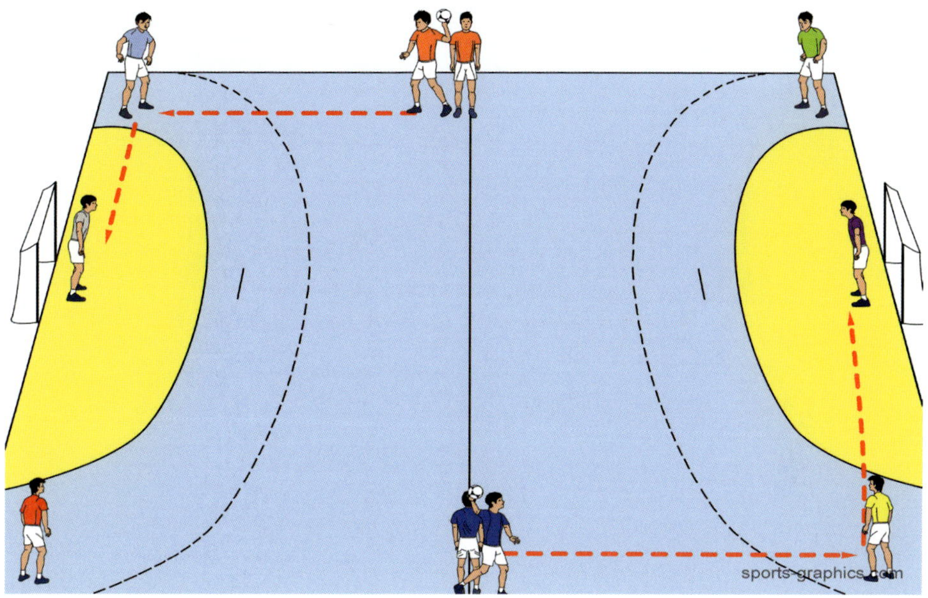

Organization

Eight players form a square by standing on the four corners and the center of the four with two balls per square. The balls are on opposite positions at the beginning.

Procedure

The two balls are played simultaneously to the right at the coach's signal. It is important that the ball is always played to the right and then immediately looked to the left; players must be ready to play at any time. Important: Do not pass while standing, but while in the pushing motion.

Variations

- The balls are passed clockwise on a visual signal.
- Change the size of the square (mark it with cones).
- Pass with the nondominant hand.
- The side centers run to the opposite position after passing. Important: Pass to the right, run, look to the left, catch the ball, and pass to the right again, etc.
- Now the corners run to the opposite position after the pass.
- Combination of both partial exercises.

5.2.3 Matching Numbers (Braun, 1992)

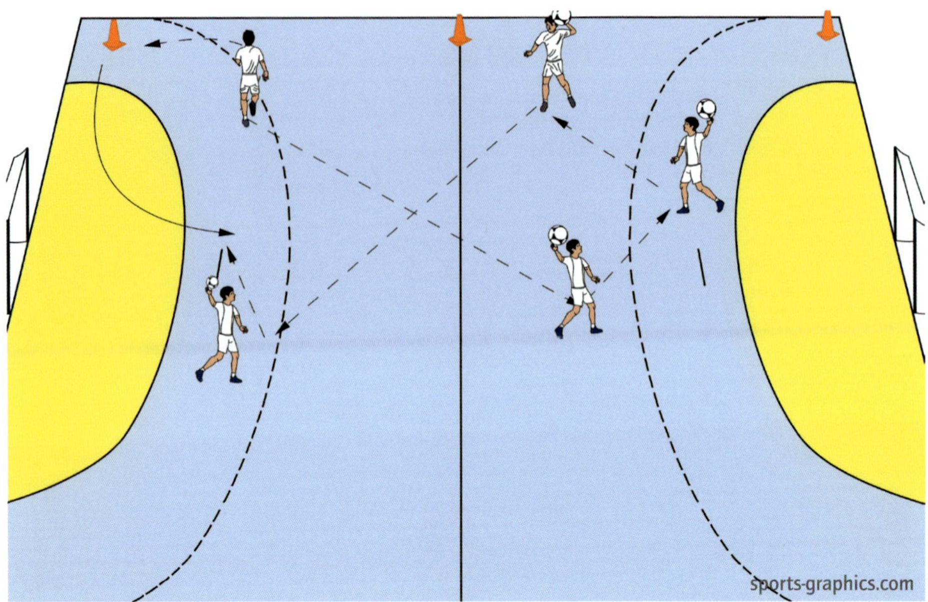

Organization

The hall is divided into four rectangles, all bordered with four or six cones or floor markers. The players are divided into groups of four to six; each group member is given a number from 1 to x (depending on the size of the group).

Procedure

The task is to pass the ball to each other in the order of the numbers (i.e. 1 - 2 - 3 - ... - x). In addition, whoever has passed the ball, runs around one of the cones or the floor markers.

Variations

- Do an additional task at the cone (e.g., stretch jump, floor clap).
- Run around two cones.
- Reverse passing sequence.
- Vary types of passes (e.g., indirect passes, overhead passes, underhand passes, change of throwing hand).
- Coach calls a number; this player bounces to an additional mat and places the ball there. Provide spare balls.
- When the coach blows the whistle, the team passes the ball to a mat. The order does not have to be followed.
- When the coach blows the whistle, the team passes the ball toward a goal and makes a throw.

5.2.4 Four-Color Party Ball

Organization

Jerseys or party bands in four colors are needed. The players are divided into four teams with different colors. The four teams line up in a square playing field with 20 x 20 m (the size depends on the number of players). There are two balls per playing field.

Procedure

One of the four teams is the opposing team. The three teams that pass the two balls to each other must do so in an order determined in advance by the coach (e.g., the ball should always be passed from red to blue to yellow).

This requires constant orientation for the players. Not only do they have to remember to whom they are supposed to play, but they also have to perceive information peripherally, aware of it throughout in order to find a free teammate of the correct color.

The players without the ball (purple team), on the other hand, move in such a way that they, as a team, prevent the passes of the three opposing teams as a team. If the three teams manage 10 passes, according to the coach's throwing instructions, the teams change, and a new opposing team tries to block the passes. If the three attacking teams make a mistake (the defensive team intercepts the ball or it falls to the ground or goes out of bounds, depending on the coach's instructions), the passes are counted again from the beginning (i.e., from 0).

Variations

- Have teams perform different throwing patterns (e.g., exclusively indirect/direct passes, passing only with the nondominant side of the throwing arm).
- Teams must use a different throwing order (e.g., blue to yellow to red, blue to blue to yellow to red).
- Vary the number of balls in the playing field.
- The defending team plays outnumbered.
- Depending on the number of players, the game can be played within the 9 meter line or half a handball court.

5.2.5 Four-Corners Handball

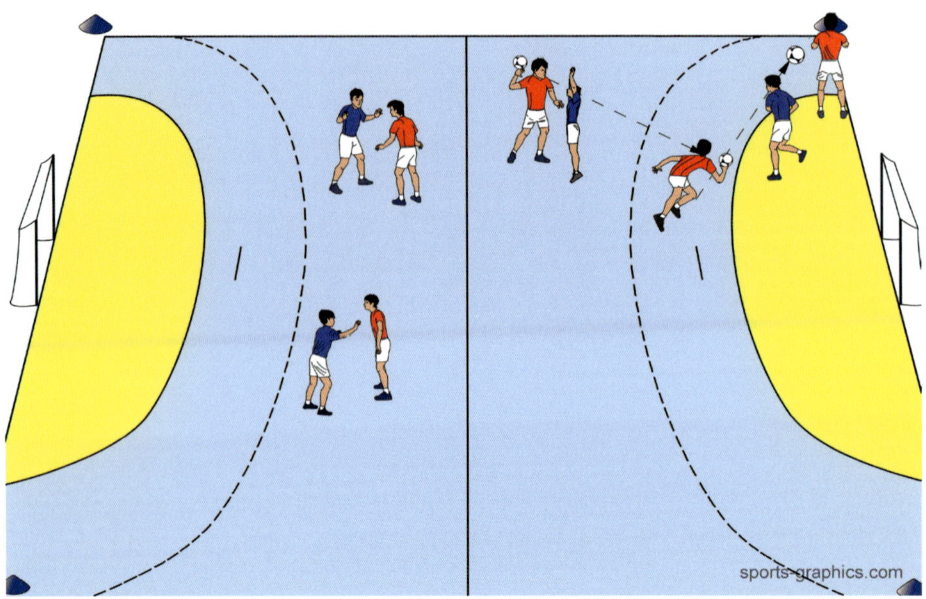

Organization

Two teams play against each other in a rectangular field according to handball rules. The aim is to place the ball in one of the four corners of the field (use a hoop as the zone).

Procedure

Open by jump, throw-in, or kick-off. Then teams play party ball according to handball rules. If the ball is placed in one of the four corners, there is a change of possession. After winning a point, the game continues from this point.

Variations

- Bouncing can be allowed or excluded by rule.
- After a point is scored, the same team continues to play until the defense recovers the ball.
- Points can only be scored by Kempa trick (i.e., the player in the air has to land in one of the hoops).
- Vary types of throws (e.g., direct/indirect passes, pass with the nondominant hand).

5.2.6 Four-Goals Handball (König & Zentgraf, 1997)

Organization

Playing field with two goals on each side (regular handball goals, mats, or similar), the throwing circle is changed to a line (6 meters parallel to the baseline) (adhesive strips). The playing field is first divided into two longitudinal strips (see green line). In each strip, two teams (of two to four players) play against each other; four goalkeepers are needed.

Procedure

In the basic form, the teams play with only one ball, which shifts the action by playing surprisingly into the other field. This requires that all players are always aware of the ball. The teams without the ball have a short break, but have to watch the other teams in case of a change.

Variations

- Teams play an outnumbered game (i.e., the respective goalkeeper plays in the attack).
- Use longitudinal line cancel; there is now only one team per direction of play, which can throw on both goals.
- Longitudinal line remains, but one ball per field is in play, which can be played into the other field. From there, either one's own ball is played back or there is an attack with two balls (not simultaneously!).

5.2.7 Bouncing Ball (König & Husz, 2018; Hoffmann, 1997)

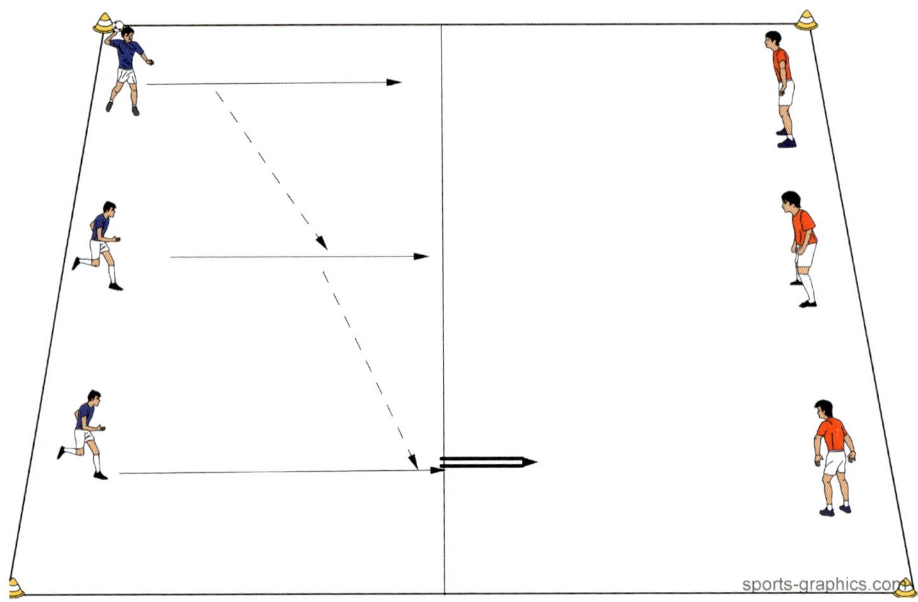

Organization

In this throwing game, a playing field (rectangle) is divided into two halves by a throwing line. Two teams of two or three players play against each other. The aim is to throw a goal with a touchdown, whereby the goals correspond to the entire baseline (cone or pole marking).

Procedure

Team A opens the game by transporting the ball from its baseline and throws at B's goal in front of the throwing line (bouncer!). All players are goalkeepers. If a player on team B deflects the ball, the counterattack starts immediately. If A scores, the ball is put into play by throwing it from the baseline (foot on the line).

Variations

- Both teams place a player at the front of the throwing line as a defender, who has the task of blocking throwing corridors or blocking throws.
- Both teams send one or two defenders to the other field to disrupt the opposing team's build-up. When their own team has possession of the ball, they go out of the field.
- This game can also be organized as net handball for jump shot training. To set up for this variation, use a volleyball net instead of the throwing line.

5.2.8 Liberation Bounce

Organization

Each player has a ball. Several catchers are color-coded. In larger groups, the game is played on two separate fields.

Procedure

All players bounce in a marked field (e.g., half field). Two to four players act as catchers (with or without the ball). A player who is hit by a catcher stops and indicates this by holding up the ball. The release is done by a teammate bouncing the ball through the legs of the downed player.

Variations

Try a variety of liberation actions:

- Knocking the teammate free (with the hand, with the ball).
- Rolling the ball through the legs and picking it up on the other side.
- Exchanging the ball (direct/indirect).
- Crawling through the legs of the prisoner.

5.2.9 Party Ball 5 vs. 2 With Two Balls

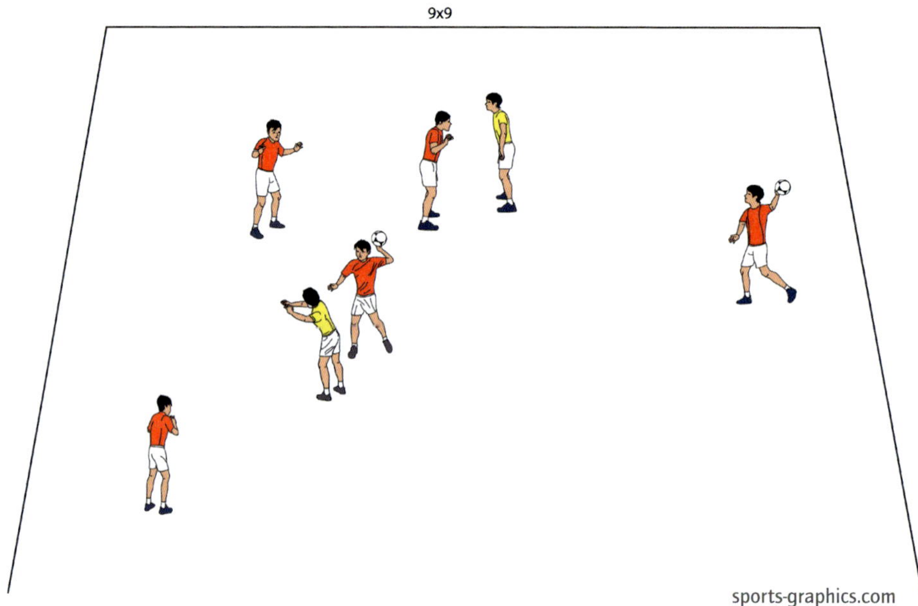

Organization

A team of five or six players with two balls plays party ball against two ball chasers who are color-coded. The game is played in a square of 9 x 9 meters.

Procedure

The team in possession of the ball plays both balls simultaneously and tries to complete as many successful passes as possible. The two ball chasers try to intercept balls. If a ball is intercepted, it is immediately placed on the ground; the attackers retrieve the ball and put it back into play.

The aim is to make as many passes as possible, comparing different teams.

Variations

- Reverse form: Time stops for a given number of passes (e.g., 20); intercepted passes do not count.
- Intercepted balls are gone. Which team keeps the balls in play the longest?
- Intercepted balls are returned, and the number of passes is reduced by one.

5.2.10 Chinese Wall

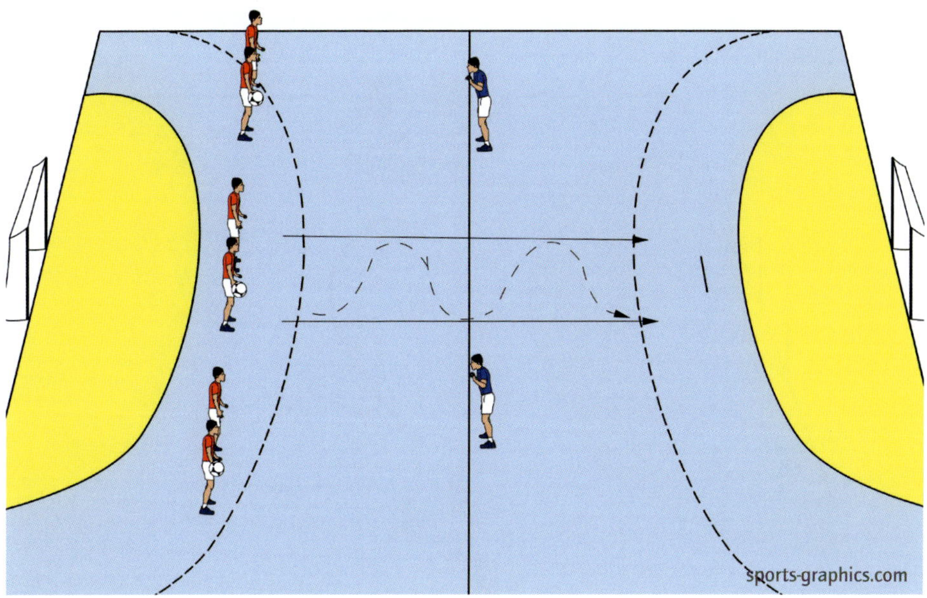

Organization

In teams of two, players gather at a baseline or in a throwing circle. Behind the baseline (in the throwing circle), there are several balls ready. There are several catchers waiting at the center line (mark them in color)

Procedure

The teams of two try to pass the ball behind the other baseline and place it there. If they succeed, they run back and get a new ball. If the action is successful, the players run back outside the playing field. The catcher's task is to stop the teams from transporting the ball by intercepting it. If a team loses its ball, it has to turn around and get a new one. The aim is to transport as many balls as possible through the wall in a given time.

Variations

- If a team has put a ball down, they run back in the playing field; if one is knocked off, both have to go back behind the discard line.
- If the player without the ball is touched by a catcher, the ball owner immediately switches to bouncing and transports the ball to the other side.
- "Who is afraid of Uwe Gensheimer?": Analogous to the game "Who is afraid of the bogeyman?", the game is played with bouncing.

5.2.11 High-Speed Passing (Sichelschmidt, 1988)

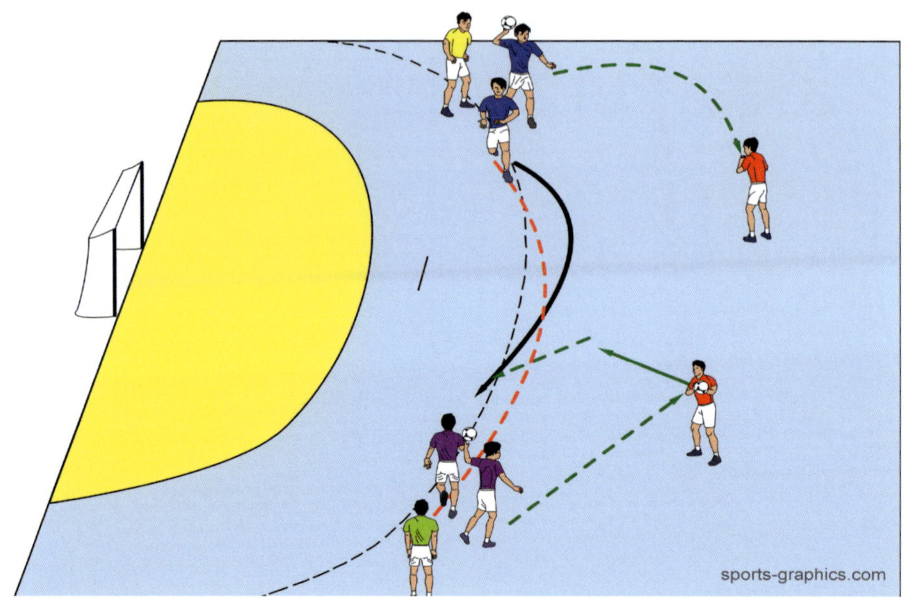

Organization

The players occupy the LW or RW position several times (line outfield). The LB and RB are also occupied. The first LW and RW player have a ball each; it is useful to have reserve balls ready.

Procedure

The players LW1 and RW1 start the exercise by passing the ball to their respective backcourt player in the pushing motion and running along the free-throw line to the other side. LB passes the ball to the incoming RW1, RB does the same to LW1. Both outside players, in turn, pass the ball to the next LW or RW and line up. Passing and running routes require a high level of perception.

Variations

- Calling for passing variations.
- Integrate FR and FL defenders: The incoming outfield players have to perceive free running paths.
- Integrate defensive players HR and HL: LB and RB backs have to perceive free passing lanes.

5.2.12 Jump Shot King

Organization

All players line up (one behind the other) at the center line. Each player has a ball. One goalkeeper stands inside the goal (GK1), the second one behind the goal (GK2).

Procedure

The first player starts, bounces once or passes the ball to himself, and takes a jump shot. While jumping, GK2 shows with his hand into which corner the player should throw. If the player hits that corner, he scores the point. If he chooses the right corner but does not score, he gets 0 points; if he chooses the wrong corner, he gets one minus point. The winner is the player who first reaches a predefined number of points.

Variations

- Increase complexity pressure through different running variations in the run-up: left- or right-hand bounce, first run through a coordination ladder, then do a jump throw.
- Cones or floor markers are placed in a zigzag pattern. They must be passed one after the other with side steps and defensive positions; then the throw takes place.
- Instead of a hand signal by GK, hold two colored cards in the corner: blue = jump shot, red = slam shot.
- Instead of dribbling from the centerline, double pass with CB and throw alternately from LB or RB.

5.2.13 Playing 1 vs. 1 From the Back

Organization

The players occupy the LB and RB position several times, one pass player each stands on LW and RW. In the defense, HR and HL are simply occupied (color shirts). All LB and RB players have a ball.

Procedure

LB passes the ball to LW and receives it back; both perform a pushing motion during this double pass. In the meantime, the defender HR has taken a clearly defensive (6 m circle, blocking position) or offensive (9 m line, basic defensive position) position. Depending on the position, the attacker decides to take a 1-on-1 or jump shot.

Variations

- Each back player completes two actions in succession: first action as above, second action with double pass over CB (additional player required).
- HL and HR choose a staggered position when in offensive position => LB and RB have to now choose specifically for breaking through to the middle or against the throwing hand.
- Competition between LB and RB: Who scores more hits in 10 actions? (Perception under pressure!)

5.2.14 Playing 3 vs. 1 and 3 vs. 2 From the Back

Organization

The players occupy the LB and RB positions several times, one pivot each stands on the right and one on the left side. In the defense, one DC stands between the pivots (marking shirts). All LB and RB players have a ball.

Procedure

LB passes the ball to RB and receives it back; in this action, both perform a pushing movement. With the return pass (as late as possible), the defender DC has taken a clear assignment to a pivot. Depending on DC's position, the attacker decides to pass to the pivot to the left or to the right.

The game is continued by RB.

Variations

- Addition of a second defender (situation 3 vs. 2): The two defenders assign themselves either to both (LB/RB: goal throw) or to a circle runner and additionally attack LB or RB (pass to free circle).
- Competition between LB and RB: Who scores more goals in 10 actions? (Perception under pressure!)

5.2.15 Game With Two Circle Runners (Duell et al., 1981)

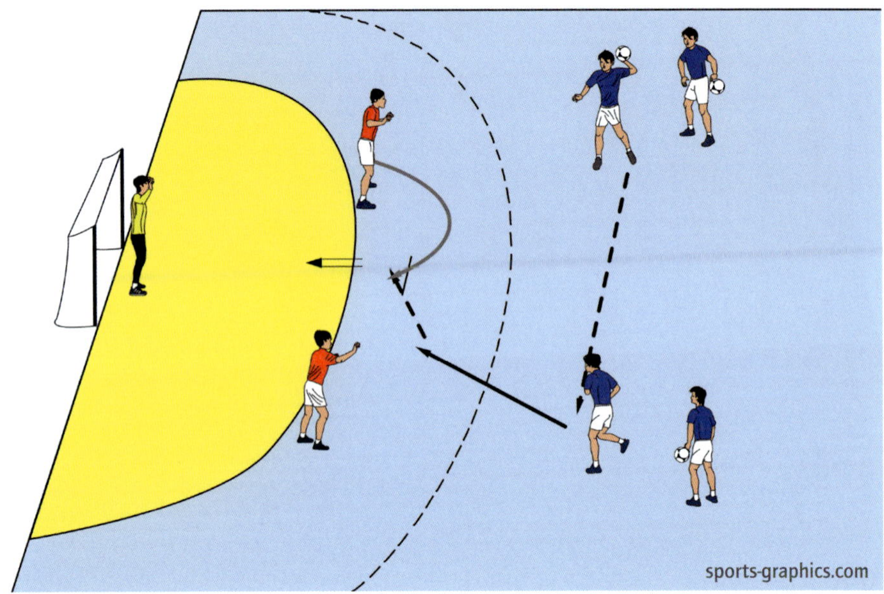

Organization

The attacking team occupies the positions LB and RB (several times). Except for the first player on LB, each player has a ball. The positions of the goalkeeper as well as two pivots (one on the left and one on the right side) are occupied with one player. Two goalkeepers can alternate in short intervals if necessary.

Procedure

RB1 passes the ball to LB1 in the dynamic forward movement. When the LB receives the ball, one of the two circle runners offers himself (short agreement beforehand by looking is necessary) by taking one or two steps towards the LB and demanding the ball (hands show readiness to receive). This player receives the ball and throws it at the goal. Then the procedure starts from the other side; LB1 lines up at the back.

Variations

- Adding further decision alternatives (e.g., goal throw) if neither the left nor the right pivot are available.
- Both pivots are each assigned a defender; the goal throw is then made in a 1-on-1 situation.
- GK raises hand => immediate goal throw by LB or RB after short dribbles to throwing circle.
- Before resolving the game situation, include several passes between LB and RB; also include, if possible, LW and RW as additional passing stations.

5.3 Games for Attention

5.3.1 Bouncing Game With Partner

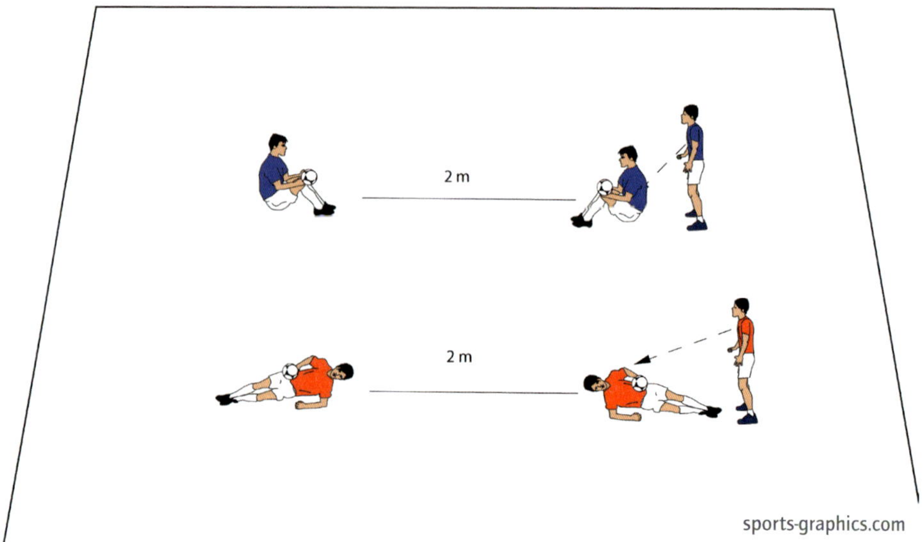

Organization

The players go together in pairs, each pair with one ball. The groups of two face each other at a distance of 2 to 3 meters.

Procedure

Player A performs various bouncing exercises on the spot (e.g., sit down–stand up, kneel–stand up, supine–stand up, etc.). Player B imitates his partner as simultaneously as possible. Change after a certain time (e.g., 30 seconds).

The players' ideas are explicitly required here.

Variations

- Change takes place on the basis of visual signals from the coach (e.g., holding up hand, dropping marking shirt, sitting down).
- Change takes place at the signal of player A (e.g., holding the ball up).
- Execution in the group of three (i.e., A demonstrates, B and C imitate).
- Execution in the group of three; now B and C take turns demonstrating and A imitates. He must always watch both of them to be able to react very quickly to the change.

5.3.2 Hoop Ball* (König & Husz, 2018)

Organization

The hall is divided into two cross fields. There are two teams of four to five players per field. There are two to three hoops more than players of a team in each playing field (example teams of four require six or more hoops).

Procedure

Two teams play against each other. A point is scored when one player plays a touchdown through a hoop, and a teammate catches the ball. The defenders are allowed to move the hoops to another place.

Each team can score points at each hoop. After scoring a point, the ball is put down, and the opponent gets the ball. Then at least one pass has to be played, after which a point can be scored again at each hoop.

The game is played without bouncing and without tapping; a maximum of three steps is allowed.

Variations

- One team can score several points in a row; the other team has to win the ball.
- Next point cannot be made in the same hoop.
- Play in tournament form; allow for short game times.

** https://www.mobilesport.ch/kindersport/spielen-reifenball-niveaus-abc/. Accessed August 25, 2023.*

5.3.3 Four-Corner Ball as King Ball (Eisele, 1997)

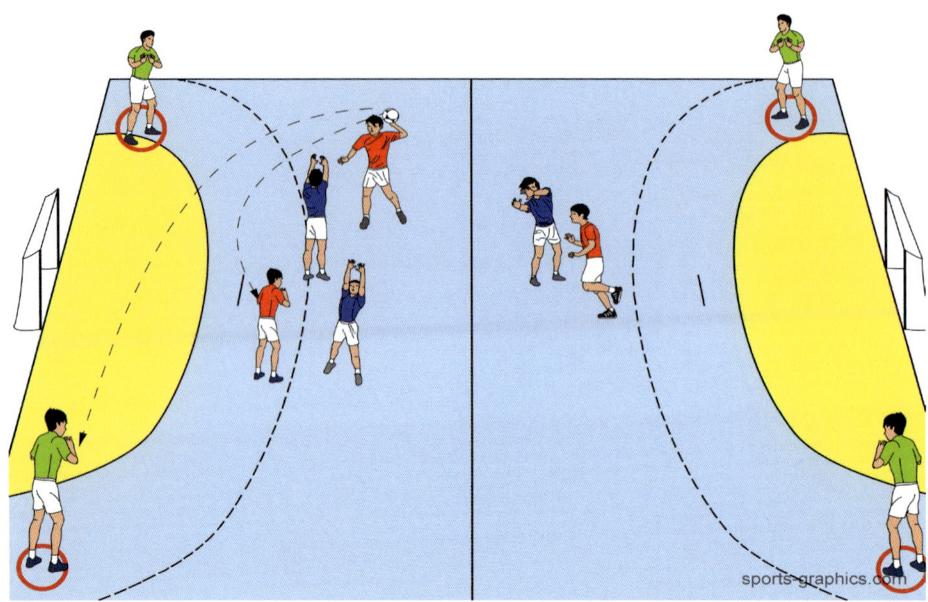

Organization

Two teams play against each other in a rectangular field; several fields next to each other are possible. There is a hoop in each of the four corners of the field. One player stands in each hoop and serves as the starting station.

Procedure

The team in possession of the ball tries to keep the ball in its own ranks for as long as possible (party ball principle), with the four kings helping out (i.e., they can be used as neutral face-off stations while the other players get some air and run free).

Variations

- Add a time limit and play as many passes as possible.
- Pass to the king only as a jump shot.
- Include additional defenders to close passing lanes.
- Kings are allowed to move along a sideline, so they can leave their hoop.
- When passing to a king, the passing player changes position with the king.

5.3.4 Each Against Each

Organization

Each player has a ball (in larger groups the exercise is done concurrently on both sides of a handball field). One group is in the throwing circle or inside the 9m space.

Procedure

Each player has a ball and bounces all over the field. The aim is to touch as many teammates as possible on the shoulder (or back, thigh, foot) and to not be touched yourself. Whoever is touched bounces to the center line, turns around, and comes back again.

For safety reasons, players should leave the throwing circle forwards and then start bouncing backwards.

Variations

- Whoever is touched bounces backwards to the center line and hops back to the playing field.
- Whoever is touched bounces in serpentine lines to the center line and back in and step-up run.
- Whoever holds the ball up just before it is touched (sits down, does a push-up, etc.) cannot be knocked down.
- Whoever is touched bounces with the nondominant hand to the center line and back.

5.3.5 Handball With Field Change (Knobloch et al., 2020)

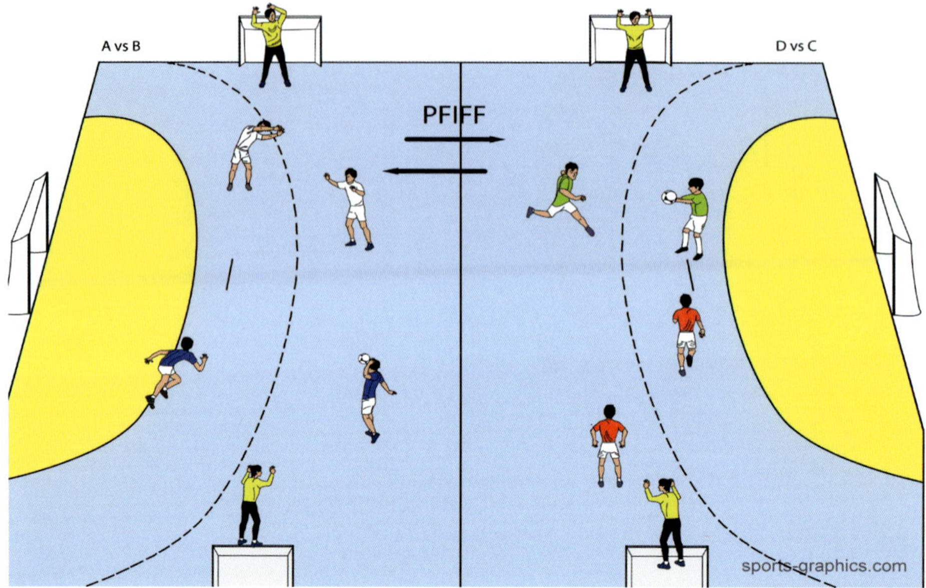

Organization

Two cross fields are marked and set up in the hall (goals). On field one, team A plays against team B; on field two, team C plays against D (2:2 or 3:3). The game is played either on pole goals (goal throws only as bouncers) or on small handball goals (or hockey goals). The goalkeepers are changed during the game.

Procedure

Handball is played on both fields after kick-off.

On the coach's signal, the following actions are realized:

- Whistle: Teams B and D change fields and have to reorientate themselves immediately.
- Verbal command "Hepp": A and C change fields.

The goalkeepers remain in their goal (no field change).

Note: If the team in possession of the ball has to change the field, the ball is put down, and the game continues from there.

Variations

- For larger groups: The player who has scored a goal changes fields and continues to play in the team of the same color; another player changes to the other side. There is no change of field for the whole teams.

5.3.6 Moving Hoops

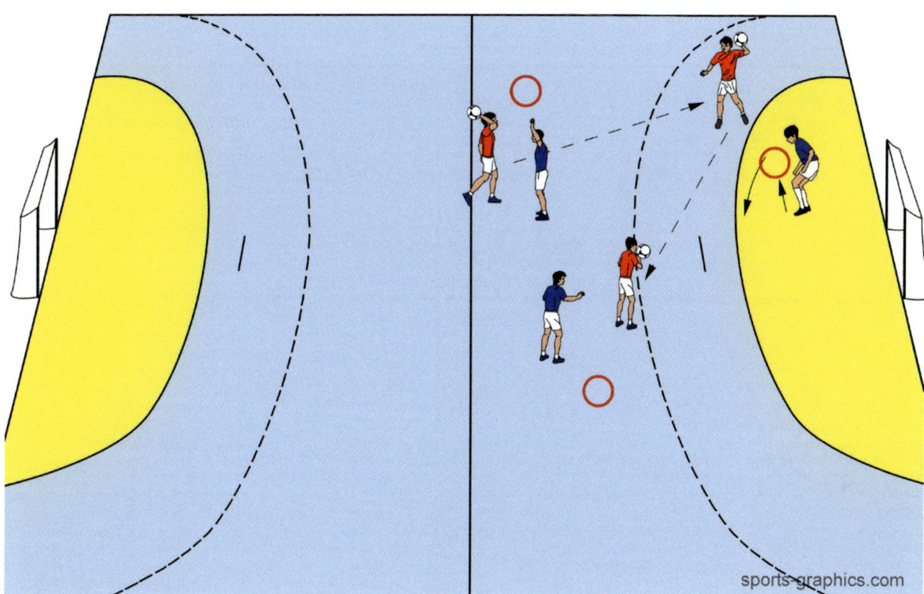

Organization

Two teams play party ball against each other in each half of the hall. The aim is to place the ball in one of the distributed hoops and to continue playing from there immediately. The defending team may move the hoops (e.g., pull them away with the feet, but not kick them).

Procedure

Opening by face-off, jump, or throw-in, team A (in possession of the ball) tries to put the ball into one of the three hoops. The defending team B can intercept balls or pull the hoops away with the shoe so that the situation changes and A has to set up again.

Variations

- Hoops can be blocked by touching them with both hands.
- Hoops may be kicked away (in this case it is recommended to choose one color of hoop for each team).
- The aim is to play an indirect pass to a teammate through the hoop. However, hoops may be moved by the defending team.

5.3.7 Three Wins

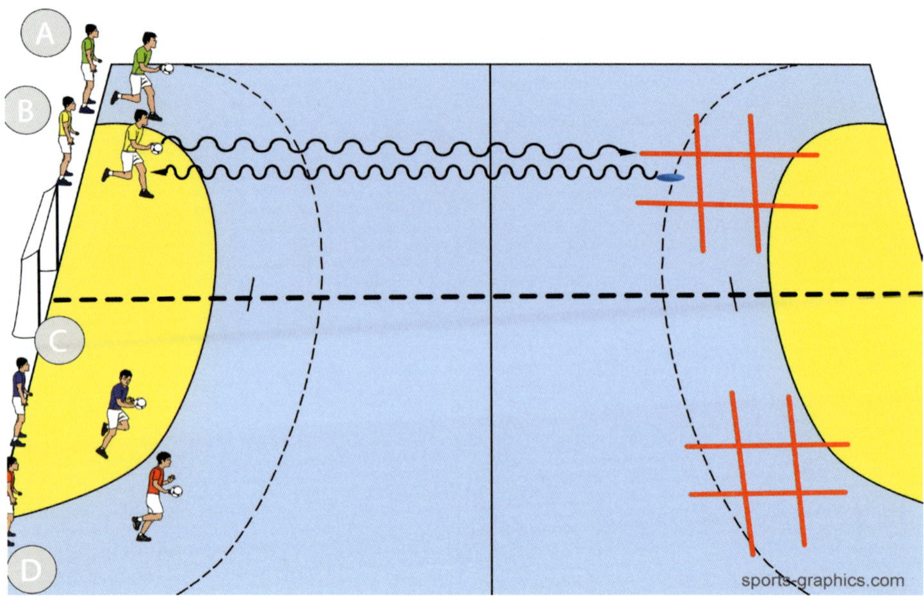

Organization

Four teams are formed (A, B, C, D), with two teams playing against each other at a time. All teams line up behind the baseline (each in a row). Each team has one ball. On the other side of the hall, the playing field for this game is taped on the floor. Each player wears a marking shirt in the team color (e.g., team A = red, team B = green, etc.).

Procedure

On the whistle, the first player of each team starts. The first player has to bounce to the playing field and place his bib in an appropriate field. Two teams place the bibs in the same field. Then the player bounces back as fast as possible and hands the handball to the next player. The team that is the first to place three bibs in a row, column, or diagonal wins.

Variations

- Increase precision pressure through running variations (left/right hand bounce, forward/backward bounce, etc.)
- Increase attention focus by changing the playing field (coach's sign): A then suddenly plays against C or D.
- Increase attention focus through team combinations (i.e., A and C can now help each other).
- The game fields are built with nine hoops or carpet tiles.

5.3.8 Two-Field Passing Game

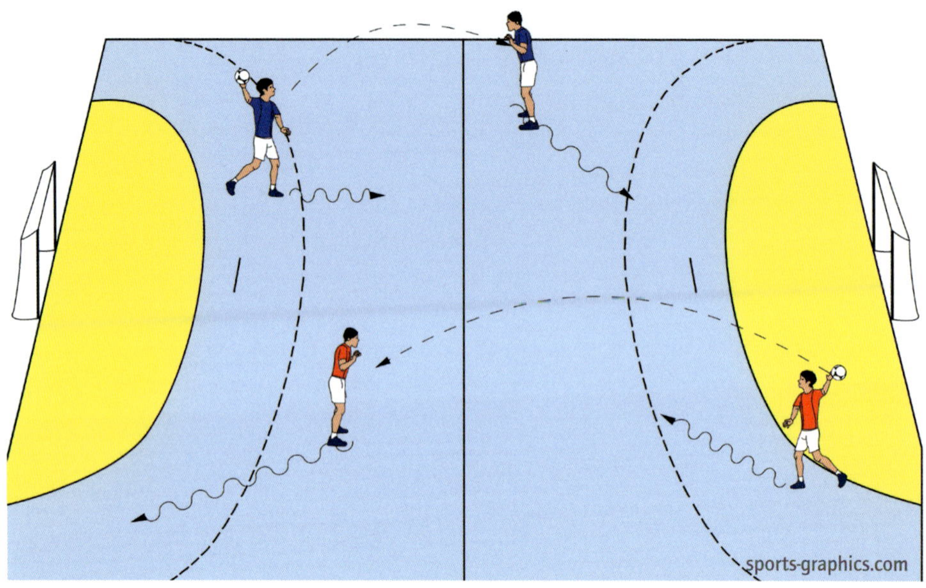

Organization

Players go together in teams of two (A, B), each team has one ball. The game is played in a rectangular field divided in two by a center line. In the simplest case, the handball field is used.

Procedure

Team A goes to one half of the field, team B to the other. The ball is constantly passed back and forth in each two-man team, with all players constantly moving freely in their own field.

Variations

- Use passing variations (e.g., jump shots only).
- At the visual signal of the coach, all players change the field, with the respective ball owners doing this bouncing.
- Additional and color-coded players are used in both halves. These can be played to if a direct pass is too difficult.
- These players become defenders who disrupt the passing game.

5.3.9 Bounce Champion

Organization

One half of the hall is divided into three equal-sized playing fields (cones, floor markers, etc.). All players have a ball and are in field 1.

Procedure

According to the principle of each against each, all players try to play the ball away from the others. Whoever loses the ball receives it and continues bouncing in field 2. The same applies to a change in field 3. Whoever remains in field 1 wins.

Variations

- Anyone who succeeds in playing a ball out in fields 2 or 3 is allowed to go back one field (e.g., from field 2 to field 1).
- The players now go together in teams of two; each team of two has a ball. Two or three catchers are determined. If a ball owner is touched by a catcher, this team has to change to the next field.
- Instead of the catchers, the teams' non-ball owners try to touch other players.

5.3.10 Stay in the Lane

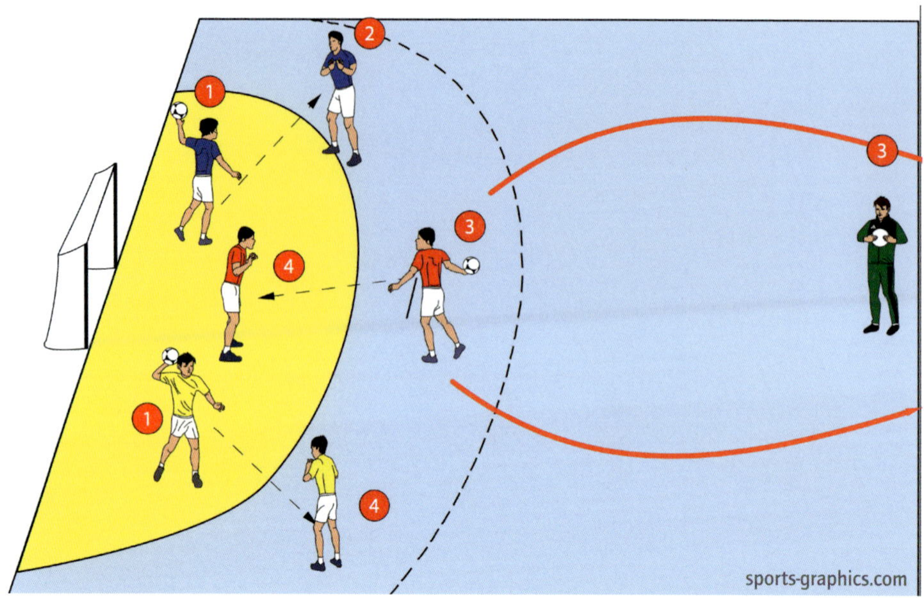

Organization

Two or three teams of the same size are formed (they should be larger than displayed in the illustration) and numbered consecutively (each player of a team is given a number, the same numbers are used for both teams). Each team has a ball and passes it to each other in the 9m space according to the order.

Procedure

While the teams are passing, the coach calls out a number. The players who have this number start running towards the other goal. If one or both of them have the ball at that moment, they pass quickly. The coach plays to one of the two. Then attack 1 against 1 or 2 on the other goal.

Variations

- Change the pass sequence on an optic signal.
- The two players called upon play together 2 against 1; this requires an additional defender in the other half.
- Restriction of the corridor for the 2-against-1 game.

5.3.11 As Fast as the Ball

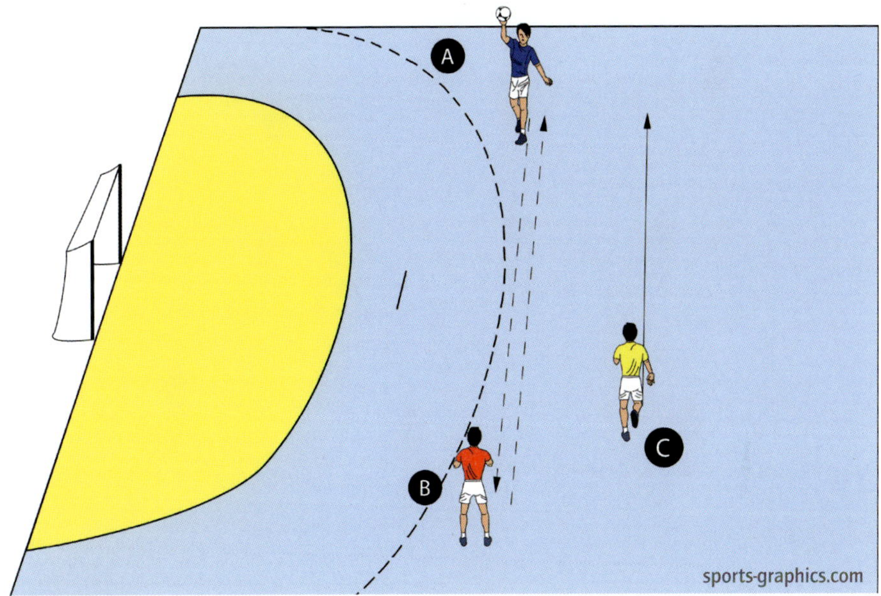

Organization

The players are divided into teams of three (or four). Each team receives a ball. Two players (A, B) stand opposite each other at a distance of 6 to 8 meters, the other(s) (C, possibly D) stand to the side.

Procedure

Players A and B pass the ball to each other at different speeds, player C tries to move at ball level (running movements or defense-specific stepping movements). If a player holds the ball up, C immediately sprints to it and touches the ball.

Variations

- Include further tasks that force player C to pay attention (e.g., A or B bounce for a short time, then C does stretch jumps).
- Every now and then A or B lets the ball drip; C reacts and runs the ball down.
- If A or B indicate a pass to C by a clear look, the latter immediately demands the ball by running towards him and playing a double pass.

5.3.12 Clamp Defense

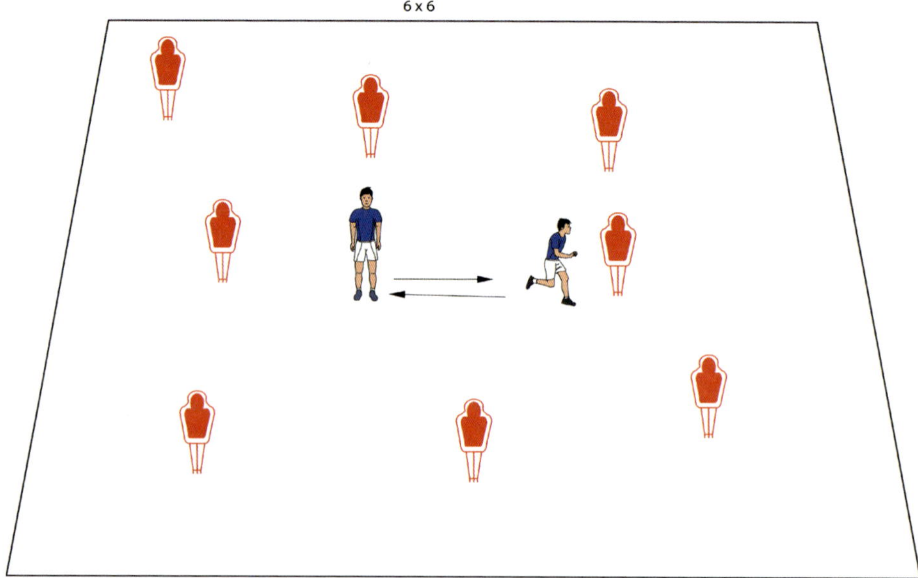

Organization

Six to eight fitlights are positioned in a rectangle (e.g., 6 x 6 meters). One defender stands in the middle of the field and moves loosely on the spot (running, defense-specific movements). He tries to keep all the fitlights in sight.

Procedure

When a light flashes, the player sprints towards it, touches the fitlight with one hand, and moves back to the starting position in defensive movements. Then everything starts from the beginning.

Variations

- All actions are performed with the ball (bouncing).
- Two players take turns (i.e., the second layer stays on the starting position each time).
- The second player moves a short distance and imitates a back-up.
- Connect with a counterattack (i.e., a fitlight has a different color; if it lights up, the player runs a counterattack, receives a pass, and finishes on the opposite side).

5.4 Games for Game Intelligence

5.4.1 Sector Game Outnumbered: 3 vs 2

Organization

The players occupy the three back positions LB, CB, and RB, in the attack. Furthermore, two defensive positions are occupied. Since the game sequences are usually fast, it is recommended that each position is occupied by several players.

Procedure

The back players should use quick passes and pushes to gain a space advantage and thus develop throwing opportunities. Therefore, relatively strict positional play should be observed. It makes sense to exclude the possibility of arced passes by rule at first. The action is concluded with a goal throw.

Variations

- Center variation (i.e., two back players and a pivot).
- Left variation (i.e., LB, LW, and pivot).
- Right variation (i.e., RB, RW, and pivot).

5.4.2 Sector Game Outnumbered: 4 vs. 3

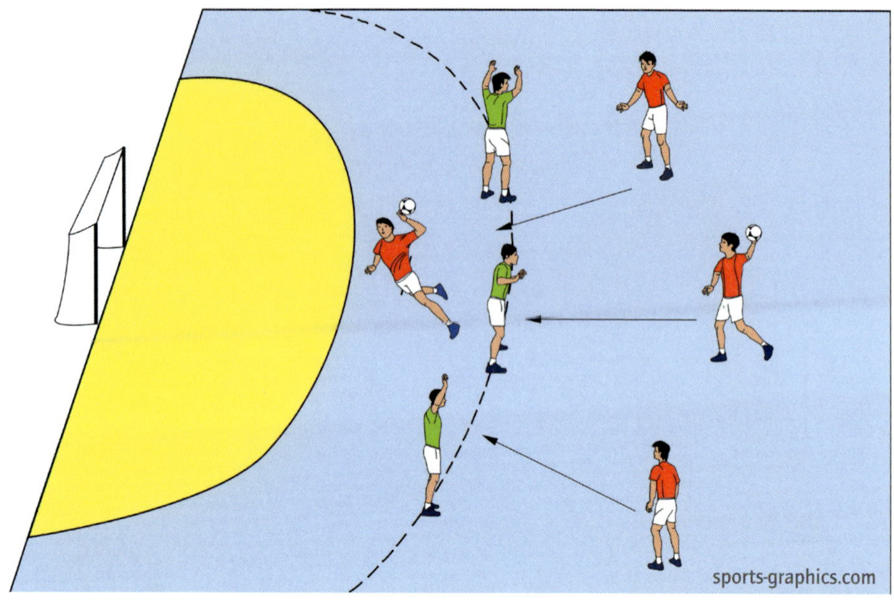

Organization

The players occupy the three back positions (LB, CB, RB) and pivot in the attack. Furthermore, three defensive positions are occupied at the free-throw line. Since the game sequences are usually fast, it is recommended that each position is occupied by several players.

Procedure

The consistent use of the pivot is important in this form of play, so simple partner aids (e.g., double pass, back pass) often arise from the game situation.

Variations

- Left variation (LW, LB, CB, pivot) or right variation (RW, RB, CB, pivot); these variations can also be practiced separately at two goals, if there are enough players.
- Play a game of 4 against 3 as threesome handball on both goals (see 5.4.5).

5.4.3 Sector Game in Equal Number: 3 vs. 3

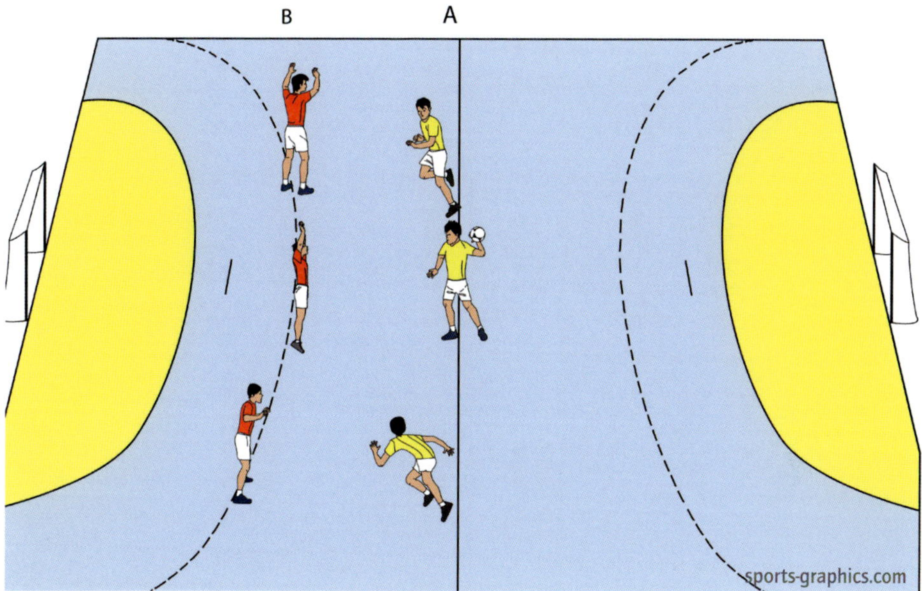

Organization

The players occupy the three back positions (LB, CB, and RB) in the attack. Likewise, three defender positions (FC, HL, HR) are occupied. Since the game sequences are usually fast, it is recommended that each attacking position is occupied by several players.

Procedure

The three back players should use quick passes and pushes to gain a space advantage thus developing throwing opportunities. The players have to learn to use small gaps in the defense.

Variations

- Variation with two back players and one pivot.
- Variation with one back, one circle, and one outside player; this variation can be played alternately on one goal.

5.4.4 Sector Game in Equal Number: 4 vs. 4

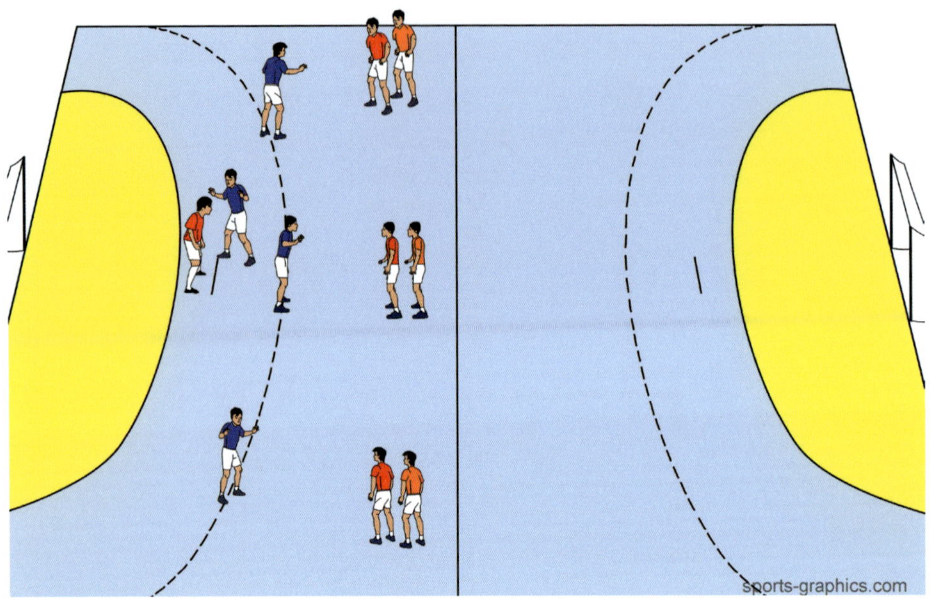

Organization

The players occupy the three back positions (LB, CB, RB) and pivot in the attack. Likewise, four defender positions (FC, HL, HR, BC) are occupied. Since the game sequences are usually fast, it is recommended that each position is occupied with several players.

Procedure

The back players should use quick passes and back passes to develop a space advantage and thus throwing opportunities. It is important that the players learn to use small gaps in the defense and to make more use of the pivot.

Variations

- The three back players act consistently with a transition (e.g., from RM). Then a throwing opportunity is played out in the 2:2 formation.
- Left variation: Attack consists of LW, LB, CB, and pivot.
- Right variation: Attack consists of RW, RB, CB, and pivot.

5.4.5 Sector Game in Equal Number: 3 vs. 3 as Three-Player Handball

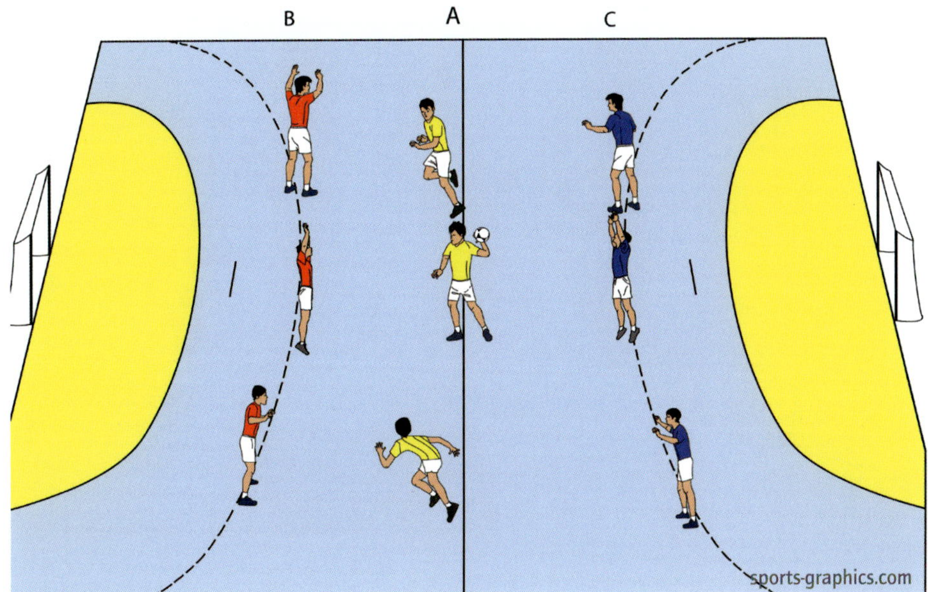

Organization

The basic idea of the sector games is extended to the entire playing field. At each throwing circle there is one team (B, C), and one team starts playing (A).

Procedure

Game on two goals, in which three teams play against each other in turn. Team A attacks against B on goal 1. After completion, team B plays against C on goal 2, then C against A on goal 1, etc.

The respective attacking team acts with various group tactical measures, especially with transitions from the different positions.

Variations

- The team newly in possession of the ball is disrupted by the attackers all the way to the halfway line.
- Extension to the game 4 against 4.

5.4.6 Mat Ball (Emrich, 2016)

Organization

The hall is divided lengthwise or crosswise into two smaller playing fields. Two soft floor mats or two blue gymnastic mats are needed per playing field. A team consists of 3 to 5 players who are color-coded. The game is started with a jump ball (as in basketball).

Procedure

The game aims to place the ball on the mat with both hands (players can also throw themselves onto the mat). The game is played without bouncing and tapping. Fast and accurate passing is desired.

Only the ball holder is allowed on the mat; the other players are not allowed to step on or run over the mat.

Variations

- Play in tournament form, according to the principle of each against each (i.e., team A against B, C against D).
- Set tasks (e.g., all attackers have to be over the center line).
- Score 5 against 5 on all fields, with 2 minutes left to play (time pressure).
- Score 5 against 5; all games end when one team has 10 points (time pressure).

5.4.7 Transition Game 1 (König & Husz, 2018)

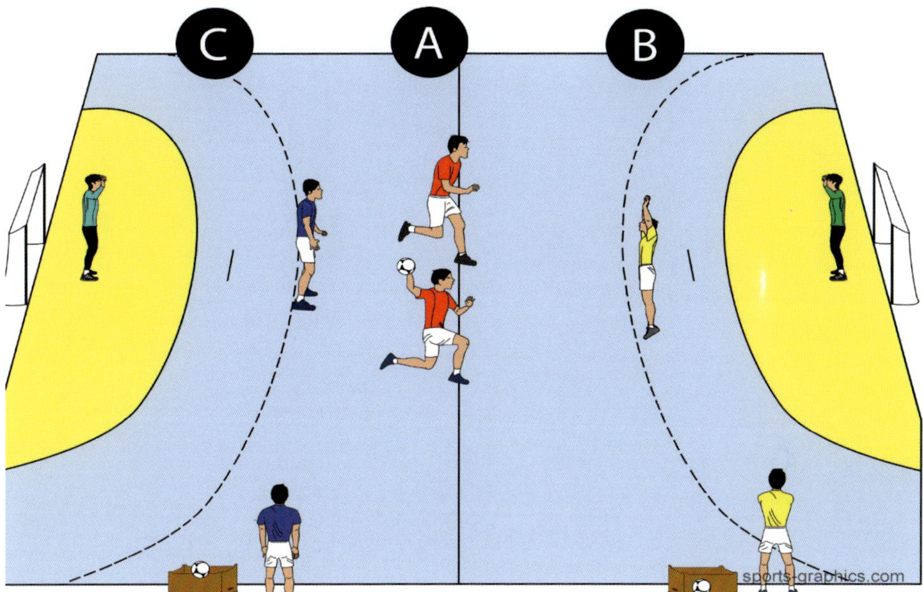

Organization

On one side of the field (lengthwise), two ball boxes are placed, approximately at the height of the free-throw line. Three teams of two players and two goalkeepers are needed for this transition game.

Procedure

Team A (red) attacks against one player of team B (yellow); the second player of B is outside the playing field next to the first ball box. Immediately after completing the attack, B2 brings a ball into the game from the outside, and team B tries to play out an advantage as quickly as possible against a player of team C (blue). Then C plays against A.

Variations

- Extend the game to 3 against 2.
- Extend the game further to 4 against 3.
- Include a prelude action of the attackers (e.g., by crossing or similar).
- Overnumbered game must be solved without bouncing.

5.4.8 Transition Game 2

Organization

Handball game on two goals in 4 against 4 (with goalkeeper). Defensive formation in 1:3, attack plays 3:1.

Procedure

When the defense wins the ball, the team immediately runs a counterattack with the three front players, player 4 (BC) secures. If a counterattack goal is scored with less than three or four passes, the team receives a bonus attack.

This form requires intelligent game decisions from the goalkeeper and all attackers.

Variations

- Consistent space allocation to the players of the first wave: left and right outside lane, inside lane.
- Change the game to 5 against 5 (i.e., attack acts without pivot, defense without BC). The aim is to bring the two outside players into the counterattack. Differentiate between the first and second waves.

REWE
psd Bank
ADMIRALBE
BGV
ADMIRALBET
DURAVIT
HER

5.4.9 Four-Player Handball (Knobloch et al., 2020)

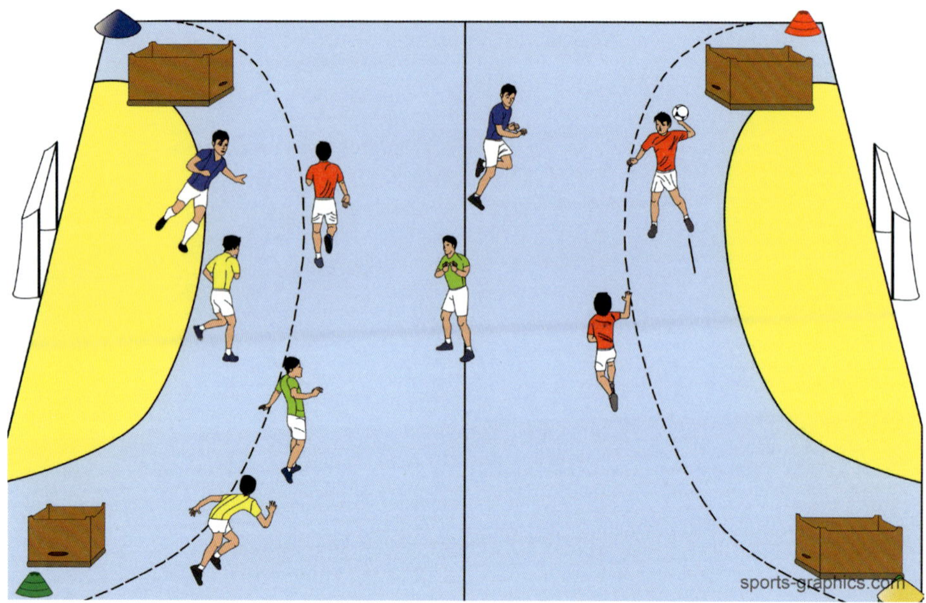

Organization

An small box is placed upside down in each corner of the hall (alternatively, use mats). Four teams are formed, which are color-coded. Each team is assigned a box marked with a colored cap or floor marker (jersey color = cap color). The diagonally opposite box is the team's second box. In the middle of the hall there is a limited playing field, where the teams initially play.

Procedure

All players run through each other and pass a ball to each other within their teams. No bouncing is allowed. When the coach calls "One!", each team must get to its first box as quickly as possible. There still cannot be any bouncing and the ball cannot be held for more than three seconds. A point is awarded to the team that first places its ball in the box and has all team members touching the box. A new round starts.

When the coach calls "Two!", the teams have to place their ball in the second box and touch the box together.

Variations

- When "Two!" is called, the team has to first run to their first box, circle it with all team members, and then place the ball in their second box and touch the box with their hands.
- Instead of acoustic signals from the coach, visual signs are used.
- Incorporate running variations and passing variations.
- Focus on bilateral training (i.e., the game is played with the nondominant hand).

5.4.10 Soccer Handball (Knobloch et al., 2020)

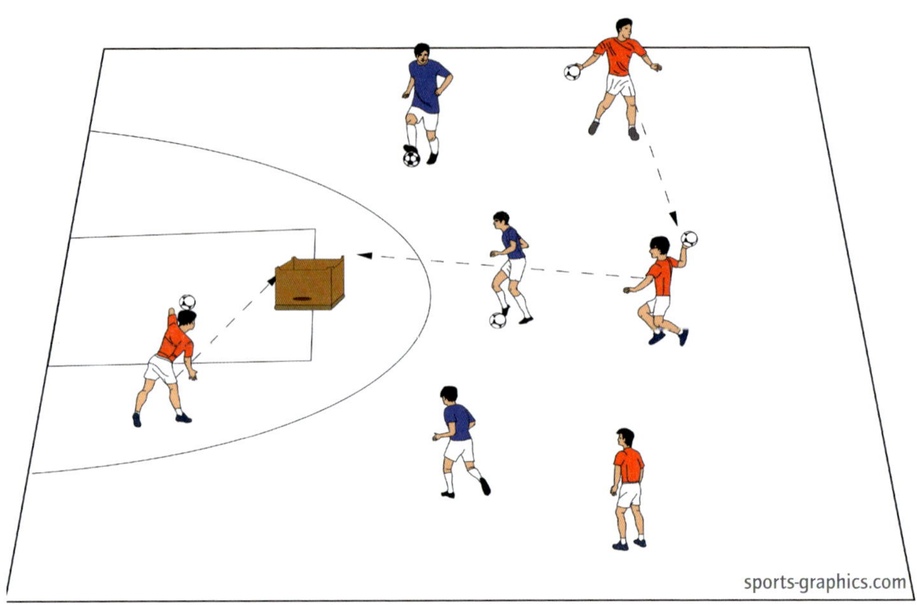

Organization

Two teams play soccer and handball on a fixed field (e.g., basketball court). Two small boxes are placed as goals on the free-throw line of the basketball court. The boxes are placed on their sides so that the open bottom (the soccer goal) faces the center of the hall, and the top (the handball goal) faces the ends of the field. The playing field is divided into three playing zones. Soccer is played in the playing area between the two boxes, and handball is played in the two outer zones (behind the boxes).

Note: The free-throw zone in front of the handball goal can be used as a throwing circle that may not be entered. Alternatively, a throwing circle can be marked with cones.

Procedure

The game is opened by kick-off, throw-in, or jump. The team in possession of the ball plays with their feet in the middle field and tries to get into one of the outer fields. There, the team immediately switches to handball. The aim of the team in possession of the ball is either to kick the ball into the box (from the middle zone) or to throw it against the top of the box. If the ball hits, team B continues the game from the small box.

Variations

- The two playing zones are swapped.
- Playing zones are exchanged on a call or visual signal.
- The coach indicates which shooting and throwing techniques will be used to score a goal.

5.4.11 Handball Header

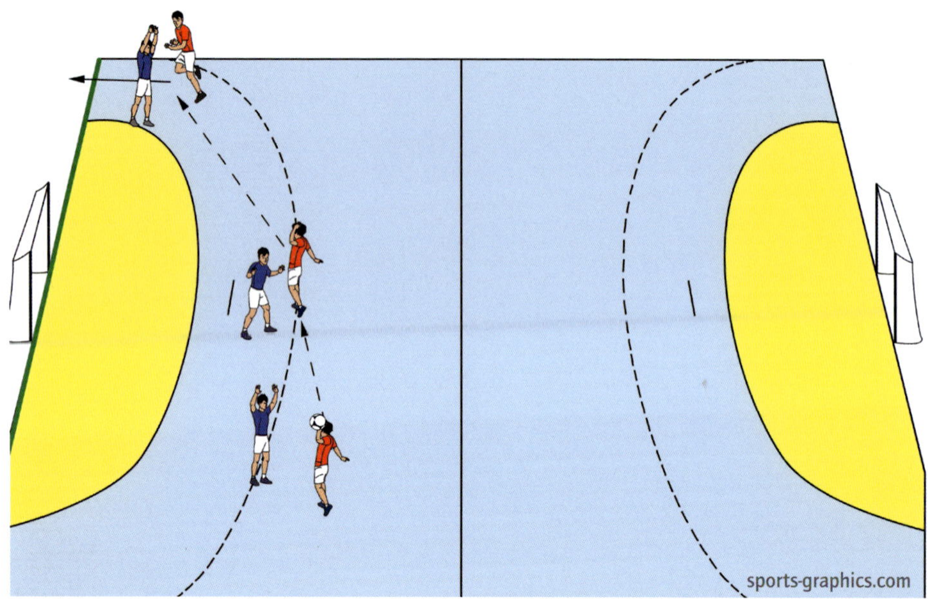

Organization

Two teams play handball headball in a handball field or half field (across). The whole baseline counts as goals.

Procedure

The game is opened by kick-off, throw-in, or jump. The team in possession of the ball plays the ball according to handball rules and tries to get close to the baseline. The goal of the team in possession of the ball is to play a direct pass so that a player can head it over the baseline. The defending team is allowed to intercept these balls and then continue playing. If scored, play continues from the baseline by team B.

Variations

- Restrict the scoring area (e.g., only two zones).
- Limit the number of passes and increase time pressure.
- Mark individual players as headers.

Kempa
AOK
Die Gesundheitskasse.
32
megawood

5.4.12 Into the Depths (Knobloch et al., 2020)

Organization

Two playing sectors are marked with cones or floor markers. In each sector there is a pivot with one defender. In addition, there is also one offensive defender per sector who defends the space between 9m and 12m. The remaining players are evenly distributed between the LB and RB positions; one goalkeeper is in the goal.

Procedure

All LB/RB players have one ball. The game is played alternately in the left sector and then in the right sector. There is a face-off player in the BC position. After a double pass with the face-off player, LB plays a pass to the circle runner who has broken away from his defender. LB uses running moves to get around the offensive defender and offers himself for a double pass. Since the offensive defender can only defend between 9 m and 12 m, LB and the circle runner play out the attack in a 2:1 and finish with a goal throw.

Note: In the beginning, the defensive defender should not interfere with the pass to the circle runner and the offensive defender should only defend semi-actively. The better the attackers become, the more active the defenders can be.

Variations

- Free play in 2:2; both defenders are allowed to defend in the whole sector, but they have to keep the starting lineup.
- Add an outside attacker who can be used as a thrower if the situation cannot be solved.

5.4.13 Two Tasks (Knobloch et al., 2020)

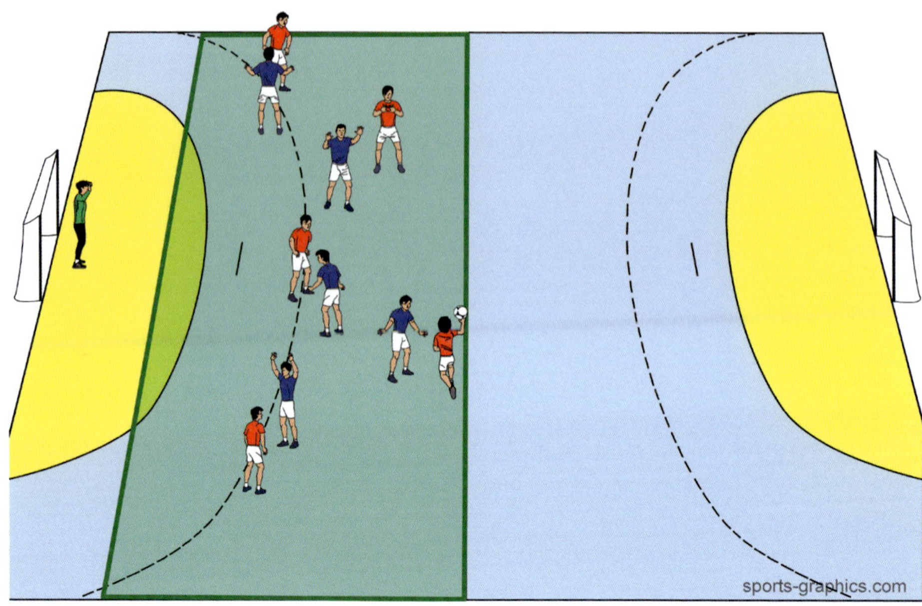

Organization

Two teams (five to seven players) play against each other on a half-field with a goal. The teams have different tasks.

Procedure

Team A (red) tries to keep the ball in their own ranks in an additionally limited field. If five passes in a row are successful, this counts as a goal, and the team retains possession of the ball. As soon as team B has won the ball, a player from A runs into the goal as a goalkeeper. Team B then tries to score a goal in overtime but can only throw at the goal inside the free-throw line.

After some time, the teams swap roles.

Variations

- Increase the number of passes.
- Limit the number of passes before a goal throw.

5.4.14 Decision Competition: LB/RB

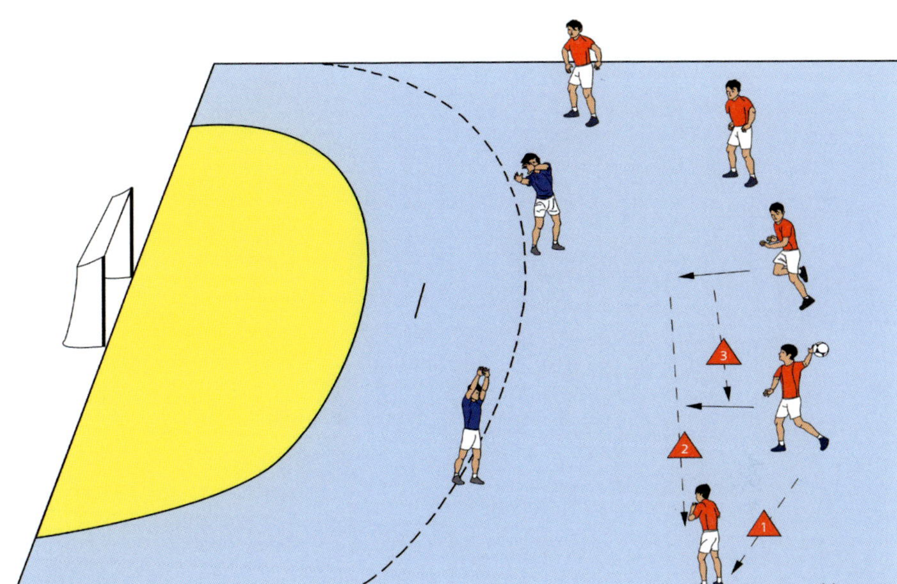

Organization

The positions LW, LB, CB, RB, and RW are occupied, of which at least LB and RB are occupied twice. The defensive players HL and HR are also in the field.

Procedure

LB starts with a pass to LW, who passes to CB, and from there, the ball goes back into LB's motion. Depending on the defender's position (defensive or offensive), LB throws at the goal or chooses the way to the circle. Then the procedure starts on the right. Each back player has five attempts. Who is more successful?

The defenders should act with full commitment.

Variations

- Offensive defense behavior means a back pass to the outside with a goal throw from there; the defender then pushes to the outside and narrows the throwing angle.
- Add a pivot. Now an offensive defense requires a pass to the circle.
- Passing is played several times. If HL/HR are offensive, passing continues. Only when a break-through direction is indicated by hand do the attackers go to the goal.

5.4.15 Decision Competition: CB

Organization

The positions LB, CB, RB, and pivot are occupied; on CB several players get ready. There are also the defenders FC and BC in the field.

Procedure

CB starts with a pass to LB, who plays back to CB. At the moment of LB's back pass, the pivot moves away in one direction. CB decides to break through to the other direction. Important: Do not forget a deception. FC can defend semi-actively at the beginning. Each CB player has five attempts. Who is the most successful?

Variations

- Add HL and HR. If the two support FC in tackling CB, a pass is made to the appropriate side. Then the respective halfback throws at the goal.
- Add another perception task (i.e., GK clears a corner, throw is made there).

5.4.16 High Speed Attack

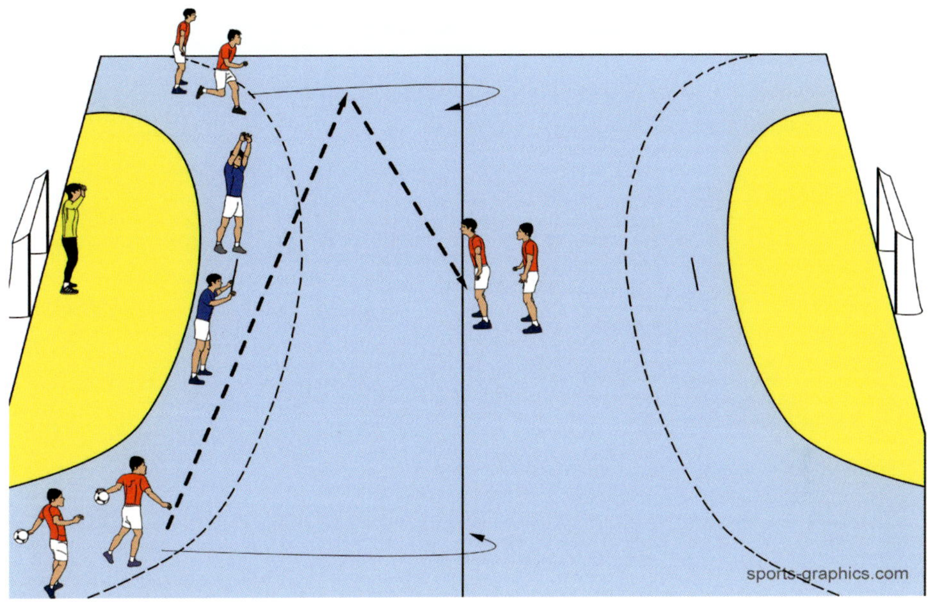

Organization

Two attackers stand in the middle of the center line facing the goal. There are several players on LW and RW. Each LW has a ball. One LW and one RW form a team. Two defenders (HL, HR) are at the throwing circle line (action area is marked by floor markers); one goalkeeper is in the goal.

Procedure

LW 1 passes into the run of RW 1 and then sprints to the center line. RW 1 passes to the first player at the center line and runs through to the center line. Now the three attackers (LW 1, RW 1, center player) play fast passes against the two defenders to create a scoring opportunity.

After completion, LW 1 and RW 1 become defenders, the defenders move to the outside, and the center player returns to his position.

Variations

- The defenders stand behind each other.
- The defense acts in equal numbers.
- The attackers have to act in a game-intelligent manner from a group tactical action (e.g., short crossing).
- In case of unsuccessful completion, the attackers have to make a second attempt; therefore, they sprint back to the center line and get a second ball.

5.5 Methodological Notes on Game Creativity

Methodical notes for tactical game creativity training can be found here. These can be used in different game forms or basic tactics.

deliberate play–In the game forms, unguided action can lead to trying out a wide variety of solutions.

one-dimension games–Game forms can train individual basic tactics across sports games through a high number of recurring, similar situation constellations.

diversification–The use of different motor skills in game forms can support the development of original solution variations.

deliberate coaching–In the game forms, no instructions are to be used that reduce the focus of attention of the players.

deliberate motivation–Hope-based instructions are to be used for the game forms, which increase the generation of unusual solutions.

deliberate practice–In later stages of the learning process, the game forms can be handball specific so that purposeful overlearning of handball-specific solution variations can take place.

5.6 Games for Working Memory

5.6.1 Indoor Beach

Organization

A team consists of five players (three goalkeepers and two field players).

Procedure

Players 1 and 2 of team A (red) attack together with player 3 (first GK), player 4, and (second/third GK) are in goal. Two players of team B are in the defense (blue), and two goalkeepers are in the goal; the third GK stands on the sidelines out of bounds. After completing team A's attack, TW 3 immediately leaves the field of play and walks back along the side towards his own goal and waits on the sideline. During team A's next attack, GK D joins the attack and TW C enters the goal.

Variations

- Game is played with only one goalkeeper in goal (i.e., two wait outside).
- Elements typical for beach handball are integrated, such as Kempa (see 5.2.5) or spin.
- Since goals count differently depending on the throwing technique, the game can be combined with arithmetic tasks; for example, each team has to score exactly 12 goals.

5.6.2 Wall Ball Complex

Organization

Two teams play against each other in one-third of the hall or fields lying crosswise or lengthwise in a third of the hall. The size of the field depends on the number of players. The two transverse sides of the playing field (hall walls) are the goals. Additional tasks are always set to activate the working memory.

Procedure

A point (goal) can be scored when a player plays the ball as a bouncer against the wall and a teammate subsequently catches the bouncing ball. If a defender catches the returning ball, it is not a point (goal).

Further rules of the basic form:

- A touchdown against the wall may only be played after seven passes have been played within the team.
- The game is played without bouncing or tapping; a maximum of three steps may be taken with the ball.

Variations

- A point can only be scored when every player of a team has had the ball.
- A point can only be scored when three indirect passes have been played within the team.
- A point can only be scored when a team has counted loudly backwards from a number X in increments of three to 0 for each attack (e.g., 15 - 12 - 9 - ....).

5.6.3 Arithmetic Handball

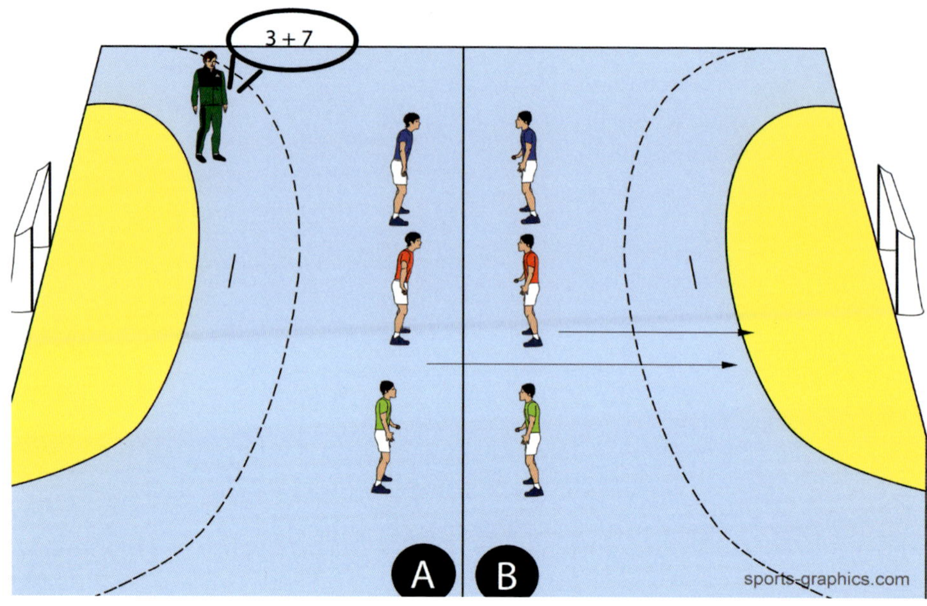

Organization

Players line up in pairs at the center line (facing each other), each two steps away from the center line.

Procedure

The coach gives a mathematical problem (e.g., (3+7)/2 or more difficult). If the result is an even number, A catches B. If the result is an odd number, B catches A. If the player who is caught can reach the baseline before the other player touches him, he gets the point. However, if he is caught, the catcher gets one point.

Variations

- Use different mathematical tasks that repeatedly present the working memory with new tasks.
- Vary starting positions at the center line (e.g., players lie on the floor, each has a ball and has to run across the baseline bouncing, bounce with the nondominant hand, push-up position, squat position).
- All players bounce and the catching action is made with the ball.

5.6.4 Counterattack Play

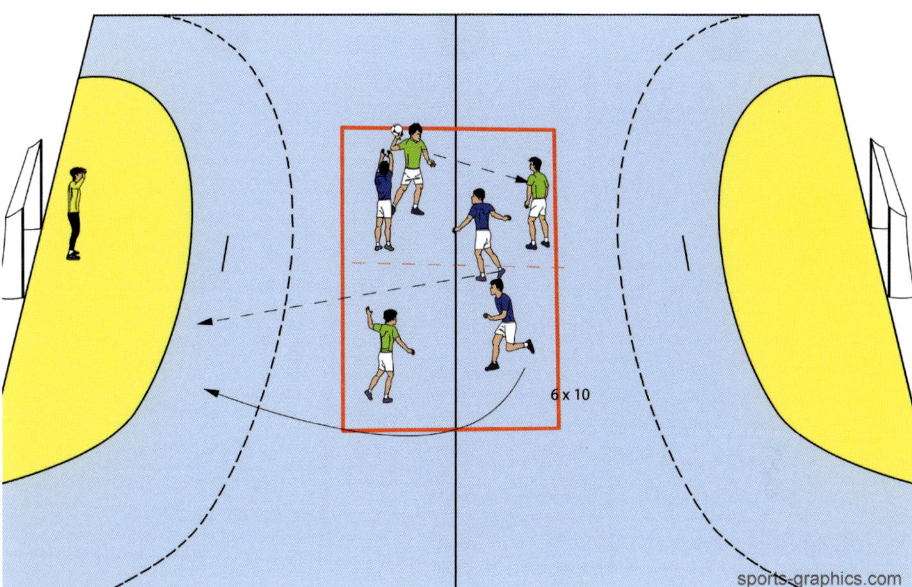

Organization

A rectangle is marked in the middle of the handball field (e.g., 6 x 10 m). In this field, two teams play drop ball against each other. As soon as one team has successfully placed the ball behind the baseline of the other team, the latter starts a counterattack toward the goal.

Procedure

The game is opened by jump or referee ball. The team in possession of the ball tries to put the ball behind the opponent's goal line after a given number of passes in the red field without bouncing. If they succeed, they receive a point. However, team B immediately starts the counterattack to the other goal.

Here the following tactical rule applies: If the ball is placed in the right half, the counterattack must be run over the left side and vice versa. Initially, the counterattack takes place without defense.

Variations

- The counterattack is run over on the same side (i.e., if the ball is deposited on the left, counterattack on the left).
- The counterattack is run over both sides and a player of the team putting the ball down defends.

5.6.5 Three-Field Handball

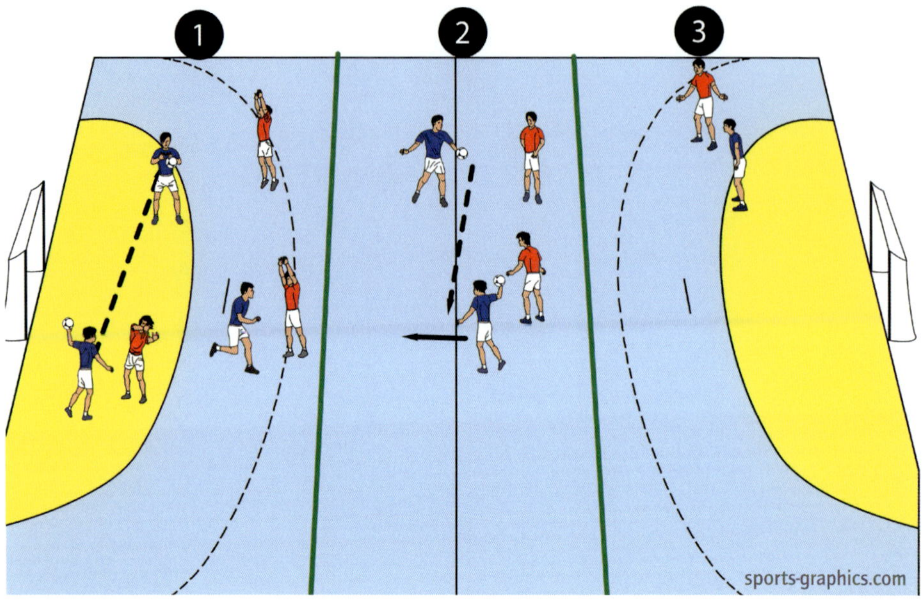

Organization

The handball field is divided into three cross fields of equal size. Two teams distribute themselves equally on these three fields. Several balls are placed behind the baseline.

Procedure

The aim is to transport a ball from one baseline to another, while players are not allowed to leave their assigned field. Points can be scored by depositing the balls behind the opposite baseline. If the defense intercepts a ball, it is deposited at the side.

Important: As soon as a ball has been passed by one team from field 1 into field 2, this team gets the next ball; however, this ball can only be passed on if the first ball is in field 3 in the meantime.

Variations

- Initially, the ball is played in one direction only. If the attacking team succeeds in depositing a ball, a new ball is immediately put into play from behind. If the defense captures a ball, it is placed at the edge of the field.

- A new ball is put into play when the previous one is in the middle field.
- The ball is immediately put into play in the other direction by the opposing team after it is put down. This also applies when the defense wins a ball.
- Begin the game with a goal throw instead of putting the ball down. The number of players should be greater in the middle field.

5.6.6 Ten Passes

Organization

Two teams play party ball against each other in the 9-m area. The goal of the team in possession of the ball is to play 10 passes and then solve tactical game tasks.

Procedure

Kick-off by draw. One team tries to play 10 passes (count out loud). After the tenth pass, the ball owner immediately runs a bouncing counterattack; the next defender follows him and tries to push him away.

Variations

- Counterattack play in superior time: The player in possession of the ball after the tenth pass and the passer (no. 9) run a counterattack; a defender fights.
- Extend the counterattack group: First the passer is added, then the passer in front of the passer.
- Create equal number situations.

11

5.6.7 1 vs. 1 Plus Line Player

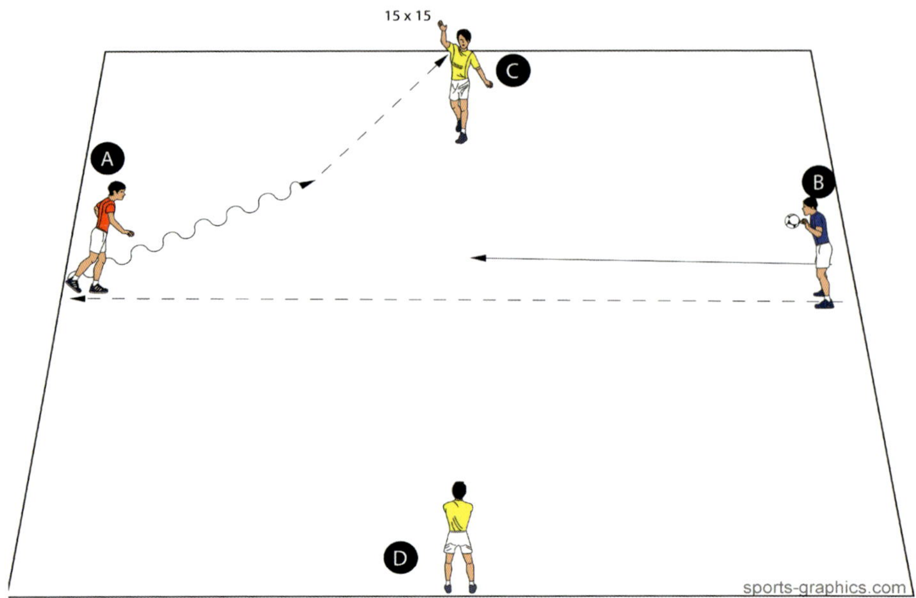

Organization

A 15 x 15 m playing field is marked out. One player stands on each side, two of the players facing each other are the wall players (C and D), and the other two are an attacker (B) and a defender (A). The aim of the player B is to bounce the ball over the player A's line, while player A tries to prevent this.

Procedure

Player A passes the ball to player B and immediately becomes a defender. Player B catches the ball and tries to get across the baseline of player A. Player B has two options to reach the goal: either to complete the distance in a 1-on-1 attack against the defender or to involve the wall players (C, D) on both sides. However, these players may only move on their respective line.

Notes

- Counterproductive instruction: "You can't lose the ball!"
- Good instruction: "Your aim is to outplay your opponent alone or with the help of the wall players to score points!"
- Bouncing errors must be prevented, so it makes sense to involve the wall players in the game as often as possible.

Variations

- Passes to the wall players are limited.
- The ball contacts of the wall players are limited (two contacts or direct pass).
- There is only one wall player.
- At least one wall player must be played to.

5.6.8 Catch Game

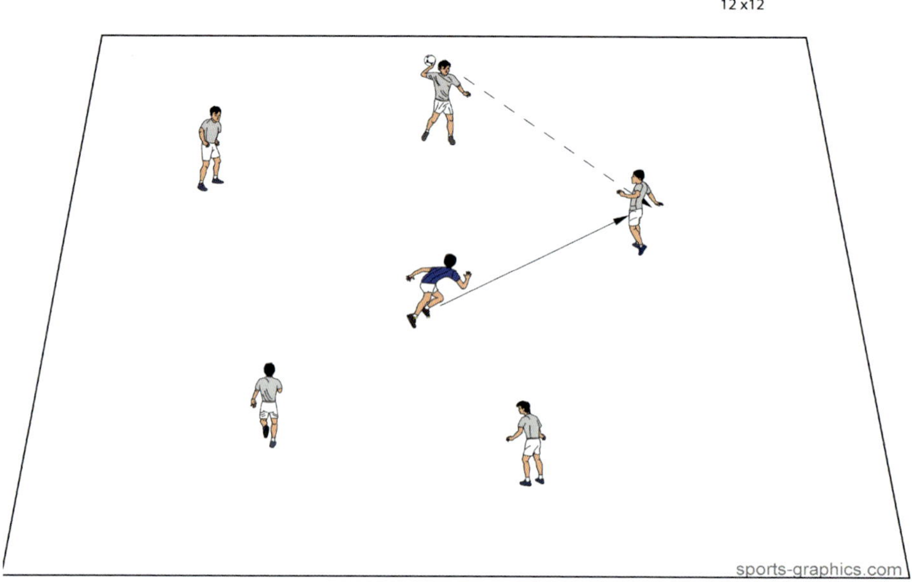

Organization

A 12 x 12 m playing field is marked. Two catchers are appointed. All other players distribute themselves freely in the field and receive two balls from the coach as a group.

Procedure

The two catchers try to catch as many players as possible within one minute. The hunted can escape from the catchers if they are in possession of one of the two balls. Players who have been caught line up with their legs apart. They can be freed by having a teammate crawl through their legs. The hunted players must pay attention to both the catchers and the players who can throw them a ball if necessary, widening the scope of their attention.

Variations

- The game ends only when all players have been caught.
- Determine several catchers.
- Vary the size of playing field.
- Players can only be freed by having a ball rolled through their legs.

5.6.9 Passing With Several Balls

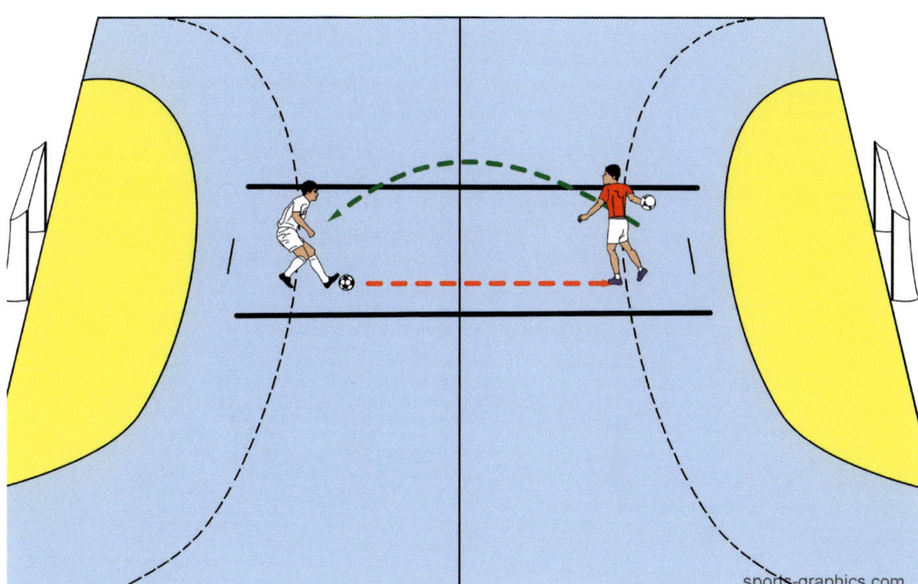

Organization

A group of any size spreads out on any playing field. Two players (A and B) face each other. Lines or floor markers designate the playing area of A and B. Each player has a ball.

Procedure

The two players throw the balls at each other according to the task. Meanwhile, a third ball is also passed back and forth with the feet. A signal word for passing with the foot can be arranged to make it easier; players focus on the speed for throwing and catching.

Variations

- Use throwing variations (e.g., one-handed, two-handed, direct, indirect, chest level, overhead).
- Consider catch variations with the hand.
- Consider stop variations with the foot.
- Focus on bilateral execution (i.e., targeted alternation of dominant and nondominant body side).

5.6.10 Number Master (Memmert, 2019)

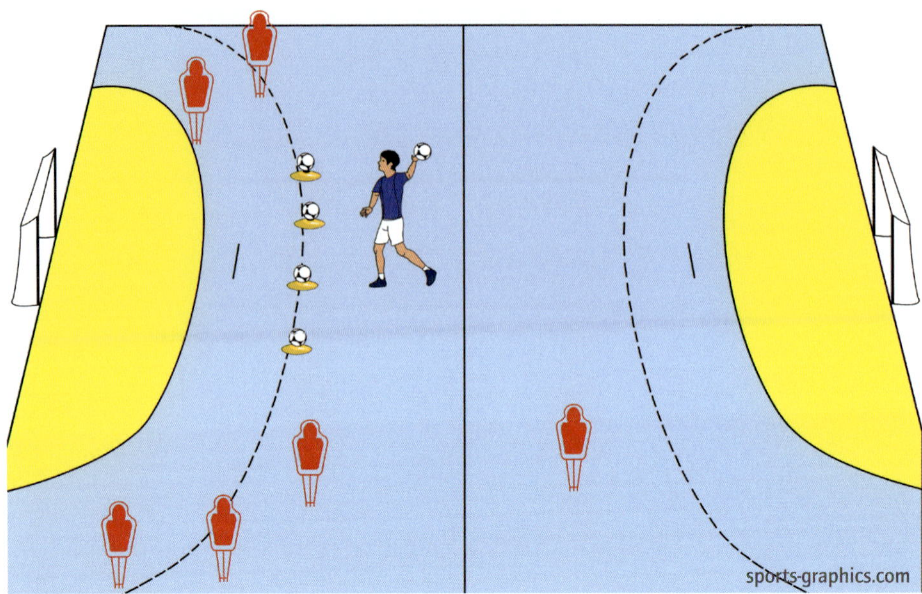

Organization

Six fitlights (with a variety of colors), six balls, six cones, and a handball goal are needed. The fitlights lie on the ground. The balls are placed on the cones at about the height of the 9-m circle.

Procedure

The fitlights light up in random numbers. The player throws as many balls at the goal as there are fitlights. The throwing technique should first be specified.

Variations

- The fitlights light up in random color order. The player has to remember them and throw balls of the same color at the goal in the same order.
- With fitlights in six colors and matching colored cones:
  - Fitlights light up in different colors; the player has to remember the order in which color the lights are indicated and throw the balls on the goal in this order.
  - A certain number of the fitlights lights up, and the player remembers the number (= ball number) to determine the sequence in which the balls are thrown at the goal.

5.6.11 Color Karate (Memmert, 2019)

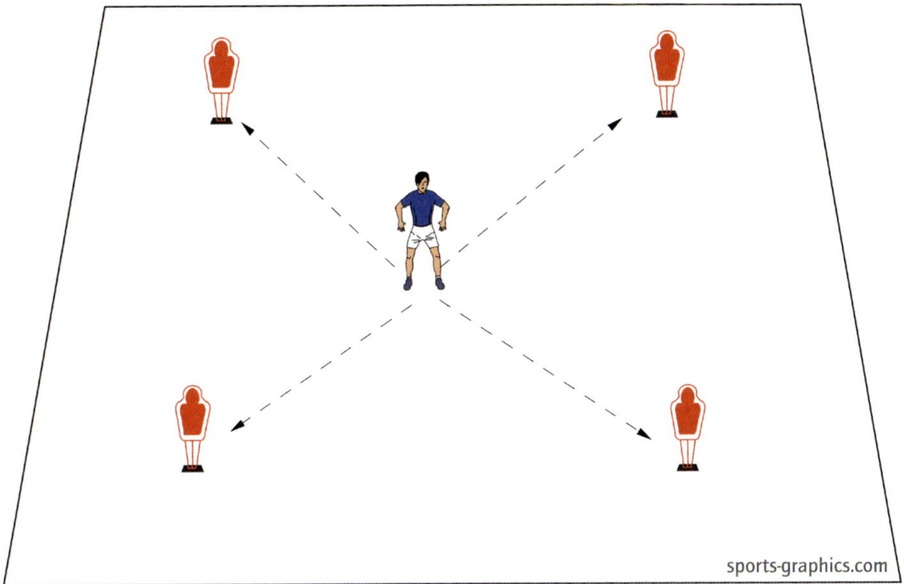

Organization

Four fitlights (four different colors) are needed. The fitlights are placed on the floor or elevated, far away from each other, according to the size and level of the player. The player is positioned in the middle of the fitlights.

Procedure

All fitlights light up at the beginning; the player turns off the fitlights in a given color sequence by tapping one after the other as quickly as possible.

Variations

- The different colors are assigned to certain parts of the body and indicate how the fitlight is turned off by tapping (e.g., red = right hand, yellow = left hand, blue = right foot, green = left foot).

5.6.12 Take Two

Organization

Twelve fitlights (two fitlights per color) are placed on the floor or elevated, far away from each other, appropriate to the size and level of the player. The player is positioned between the fitlights.

Procedure

All twelve lights go on together. The player should always turn off the same colors one after the other by tapping with either his foot or hand.

Variations

- One fitlight should be turned off with the left part of the body and the other fitlight of the same color with the right part of the body.
- The fitlights of the same color should be turned off at the same time. Fitlights have to then lie closely in a circle around the player.

5.6.13 Burpee King (Memmert, 2019)

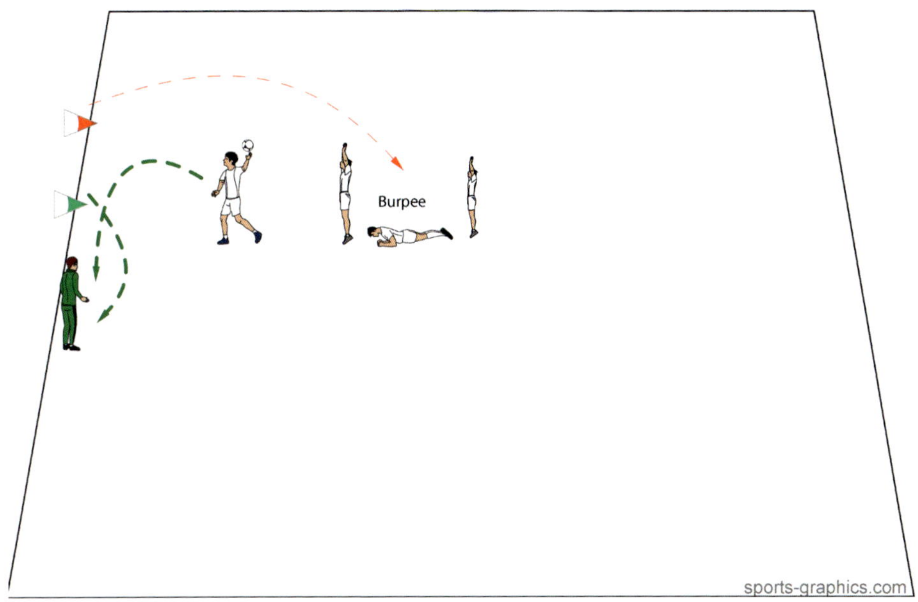

Organization

Two fitlights (set to the same color) are fixed to the wall. One light is positioned directly in front of the player; the other is fixed to the left or right of the wall in front of the player. The player stands a few meters away from the wall with the ball in his hand.

Procedure

If the light shines directly in front of the player, he throws the ball against the wall in front of him, if the light shines to the left or right of him, the player passes the ball to the coach or a teammate and performs a burpee.

Variations

- Other tasks, such as push-ups, stretch jumps, or similar, can be added.
- The coach or partner shows a number between 1 and 4; this corresponds to the number of repetitions of burpees (or other task).
- The coach or partner gives a simple arithmetic problem (e.g., 8+4). The result corresponds to the number of repetitions to be performed.

5.6.14 Quadrant Ball (Knobloch et al., 2020)

Organization

Half a handball field is divided into four squares (10 x 10 m). Teams of two are formed and distributed among the quadrants.

Procedure

Two teams play against each other in a field consisting of four quadrants. In this party ball game, the players pass the ball to each other within their team. The change of possession of the ball is possible by winning the ball. The aim is to bounce after receiving the ball to reach the next square to pass the ball. After ten passes, the team gets a point, and the other team gets the ball.

Variations

- Vary the number of passes per square.
- Pass into another quadrant and follow up.

5.6.15 Zone Change Ball (Knobloch et al., 2020)

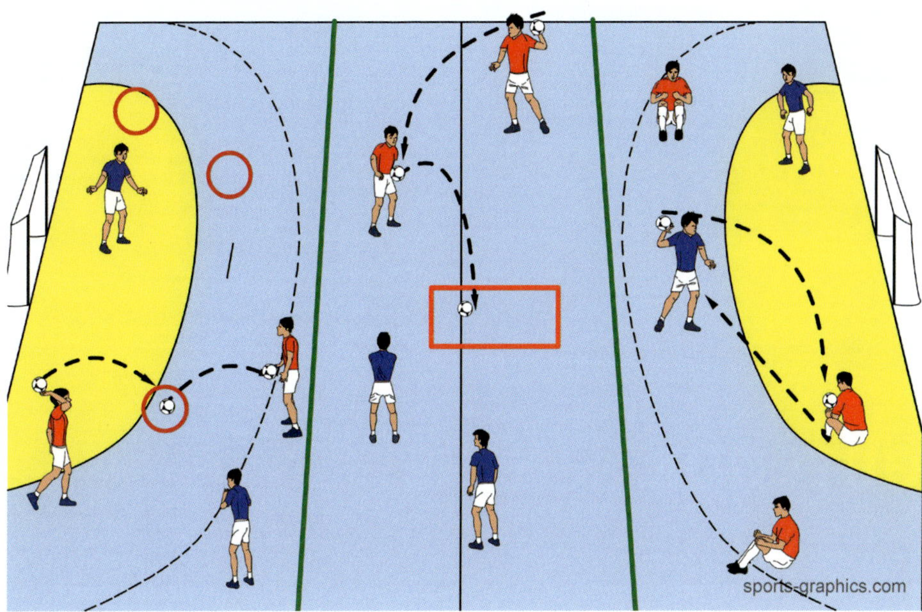

Organization

The handball field is divided into three zones. There are different tasks to be solved per small playing field. In each case two teams act against each other. Tasks:

- Zone 1: Ground pass through a hoop to teammate.
- Zone 2: Place ball in rectangle (on a mat).
- Zone 3: Double pass with a player sitting on the floor.

Procedure

Team A starts and has three attempts to score a point; this applies to all zones. If team B captures the ball, they continue to play. After a short period of time, the team changes; this is done on the coach's signal.

Variations

- Perform the tasks with and without bouncing.
- Vary the tasks in the three fields.

OUTLOOK

Currently, the title *creative player* is considered a high distinction for handball players and increases their market value enormously, as this species still seems to be rare. For example, the players on the left and right backs in handball have the task of shaping the attacking play of a team variably through cleverness and, above all, game intelligence, but also, perhaps surprisingly, creative decision-making behavior, while the players on the center back position are supposed to prepare the finishing opportunities of their teammates with creative solutions.

In the German Handball Bundesliga, rankings are repeatedly compiled in which the best German junior players are selected and awarded with prizes. Nevertheless, it is surprising that only about 35% of these former top talents manage to get a regular spot at one of the 18 Bundesliga clubs and thus make the breakthrough into the professional ranks. One reason could be that the selection is based more on physical and technical factors and less on cognitive factors such as attention, game intelligence, and creativity.

Structured according to the integrative framework model for decision-making (cf. figure 1), after the introductory theoretical explanations on the individual cognitions (anticipation, perception, attention, game intelligence, game creativity, working memory), diagnostic tools and countless game, competition, and practice forms were presented that have proven themselves in practice. The framework model having been described can help coaches and trainers to plan and execute training in a systematic and focused way, to set priorities or to work on identified deficits. The cognitions described can be taken into account and specifically promoted in every age range (i.e., in children's, youth, or adult training) as well as at all performance levels (from beginner to professional). This can be understood as an ongoing process that can also be integrated into training blocks of clubs and associations.

On the basis of specific training measures and practical exercise forms, all facets of cognition can be trained profitably in training. Not only in competitive sports, but also in children's and early youth training, cognitions should be given more attention in the training and education process.

In our opinion, everyday practice has not yet recognized the potential of training handball-specific cognitions, and uses already gained knowledge too little. We still have a certain knowledge deficit here. It can be predicted today that in five to ten years cognition will be a central component of talent diagnostics, selection procedures, training control, and training content from the junior to the professional level.

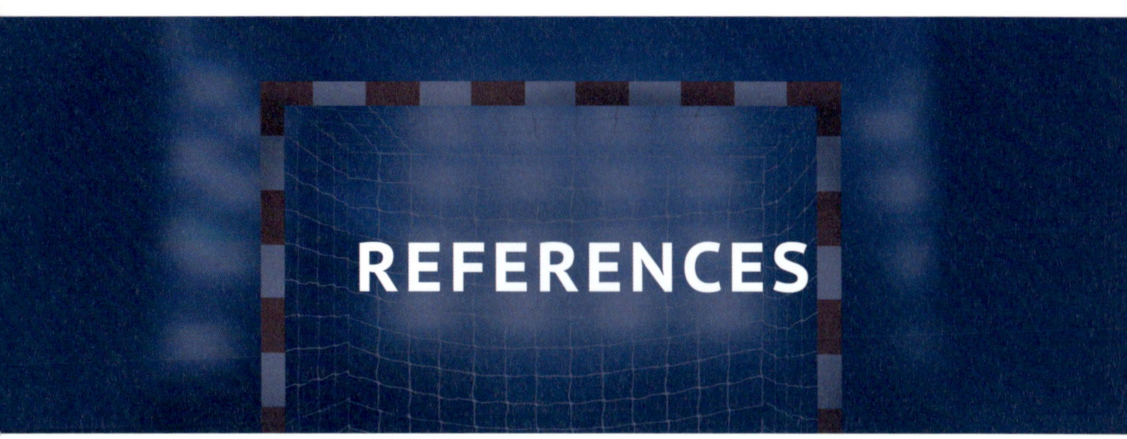

REFERENCES

Abernethy, B. & Russell, D. G. (1987). Expert-novice differences in an applied selective attention task. *Journal of Sport Psychology, 9*(4), 326–345.

Abernethy, B., Maxwell, J. P., Masters, R. S. W., van der Kamp, J., & Jackson, R. C. (2007). Attentional processes in skill learning and expert performance. In G. Tenenbaum & R. C. Eklund (Eds.), *Handbook of Sport Psychology* (3rd ed.). Wiley & Sons.

Abernethy, B., Schorer, J., Jackson, R. C., & Hagemann, N. (2012). Perceptual training methods compared: The relative efficacy of different approaches to enhancing sport-specific anticipation. *Journal of Experimental Psychology: Applied, 18*(2), 143.

Alhosseini, Z. N., Safavi, S., & Namazi, M. (2015). Effect of visual search and skill-level on the spatial occlusion anticipation in handball players. *International Journal of Sports Sciences & Fitness, 5*(1). 1–18.

Alvarez, G. A., & Franconeri, S. L. (2005). How many objects can you track? Evidence for a flexible tracking resource. *Journal of Vision, 5*, 641–641.

Alvarez, J. A., & Emory, E. (2006). Executive function and the frontal lobes: a meta-analytic review. *Neuropsychology Review, 16*, 17–42.

Augste, C. (2006). *Techniktraining und konditionelle Belastungen. Eine Untersuchung zum Wurftraining mit Jugendlichen im Basketball.* Sportverlag Strauß.

Baddeley, A. D. (2007). *Working memory, thought, and action.* Oxford University Press.

Bakker, F. C., Oudejans, R. D., Binsch, O., & van der Kamp, J. (2006). Penalty taking and gaze behavior: Unwanted effects of the wish not to miss. *International Journal of Sport Psychology, 37*, 265–280.

Beck, D. M., & Lavie, N. (2005). Look here but ignore what you see: Effects of distractors at fixation. *Journal of Experimental Psychology: Human Perception and Performance, 31*(3), 592-607.

Benedek, M., Jauk, E., Sommer, M., Arendasy, M., & Neubauer, A. C. (2014). Intelligence, creativity and cognitive control: The common and differential involvement of executive functions in intelligence and creativity. *Intelligence, 46*(1), 73-83.

Bideau, B., Multon, F., Kulpa, R., Fradet, L., Arnaldi, B., & Delamarche, P. (2004). Using virtual reality to analyze links between handball thrower kinematics and goalkeeper's reactions. *Neuroscience Letters, 372*(1-2), 119-122.

Bishop, D. T., Wright, M. J., Jackson, R. C., & Abernethy, B. (2013). Neural bases for anticipation skill in soccer: An FMRI study. *Journal of Sport & Exercise Psychology, 35*(1), 98-109.

Bourne, M., Bennett, S. J., Hayes, S. J., & Williams, A. M. (2011). The dynamical structure of handball penalty shots as a function of target location. *Human Movement Science, 30*(1), 40-55.

Bourne, M., Bennett, S. J., Hayes, S. J., Smeeton, N. J., & Williams, A. M. (2013). Information underpinning anticipation of goal-directed throwing. *Attention, Perception, & Psychophysics, 75*(7), 1559-1569.

Brack, R., & Bauer, J. (2019/2020). 6 gegen 7 verteidigen - kreativ und intelligent. Eine aktiv-antizipative Abwehrphilosophie. *Handballtraining 39*(12), 32-39 (I), *40*(3), 26-39 (II), *40*(8), 24-31 (III).

Braun, R. (1992). Zahlenspielreihe. *Rebound - Organ des Basketballverbandes Baden-Württemberg*, 2, 26-30.

Broadbent, D. E. (1958). *Perception and communication.* Pergamon Press.

Bruce, V., Green, P., & Georgeson, M. (1996). *Visual perception. Physiology, psychology and ecology* (3rd ed.). Psychology Press.

Cañal-Bruland, R., van der Kamp, J., & van Kesteren, J. (2010). An examination of motor and perceptual contributions to the recognition of deception from others' actions. *Human Movement Science, 29*, 94-102. https://doi.org/10.1016/j.humov.2009.10.001

Cavanagh, P., & Alvarez, G.A. (2005). Tracking multiple targets with multifocal attention. *Trends in Cognitive Sciences, 9*(7), 349-354.

Cocić, D., Vaci, N., Prieger, R., & Bilalić, M. (2020). Reading the future from body movements-anticipation in handball. *Journal of Motor Behavior*, 1-16.

Cohen, M. A., Nakayama, K., Konkle, T., Stantic, M., & Alvarez, G. A. (2015). Visual awareness is limited by the representational architecture of the visual system. *Journal of Cognitive Neuroscience, 27*, 2240–2252.

Conway, A. R. A., Jarrold, C., Kane, M. J., Miyake, A., & Towse, J. N. (2007). *Variation in working memory.* Oxford University Press.

Conway, A. R., Kane, M. J., Bunting, M. F., Hambrick, D. Z., Wilhelm, O., & Engle, R. W. (2005). Working memory span tasks: A methodological review and user's guide. *Psychonomic Bulletin & Review, 12*, 769–786.

Côté, J., Baker, J., & Abernethy, B. (2007). Practice and play in the development of sport expertise. In G. Tenenbaum & R. C. Eklund (Eds.), *Handbook of Sport Psychology* (pp. 184–202). Wiley.

Coull, J. T. (1998). Neural correlates of attention and arousal: Insights from electrophysiology, functional neuroimaging and psychopharmacology. *Progress in Neurobiology*, 55(4), 343–361.

Cowan, N. (1995) *Attention and memory: An integrated framework.* Oxford University Press.

Cowan, N. (2001). The magical number 4 in short-term memory: A reconsideration of mental storage capacity. *Behavioral and Brain Sciences, 24*, 87–185. https://doi.org/10.1017/S0140525X01003922

Cowan, N. (2005). *Working memory capacity.* Psychology Press.

Crone, E. A., Wendelken, C., Donohue, S., van Leijenhorst, L., & Bunge, S. A. (2006). Neurocognitive development of the ability to manipulate information in working memory. *Proceedings of the National Academy of Sciences, 10*, 9315–9320.

De Sa Fardilha, F., & Allen, J. (2019). Defining, assessing, and developing creativity in sport: A systematic narrative review (Forthcoming/Available Online). *International Review of Sport and Exercise Psychology.* https://doi.org/10.1080/1750984X.2019.1616315

Debanne, T. (2014). Techniques used by coaches to influence referees in professional team handball. *International Journal of Sports Science & Coaching, 9*(3), 433–446.

Debanne, T., & Laffaye, G. (2015). Motivational cues predict the defensive system in team handball: A model based on regulatory focus theory. *Scandinavian Journal of Medicine & Science in Sports, 25*(4), 558–567.

Diamond, A. (2013). Executive functions. *Annual Review of Psychology, 64*, 135–168.

Dietrich, K. (1984). Vermitteln Spielreihen die Spielfähigkeit? *Sportpädagogik, 8*(1), 19-21.

Döbler, H. (1964). Die Systematik der Spiele als Grundlage einer vergleichenden sportpädagogischen Betrachtung. *Theorie und Praxis der Körperkultur, 13*, 217-31.

Dreckmann, C., & Görsdorf, K. (2010). *Qualitative Spielbeobachtung 2.0: Ein qualitativ-evaluatives Verfahren zur Verbesserung der Kommunikationsbedingungen im Handball unter dem Fokus der Generierung optimaler Vermittlungsstrategien für taktische Informationen und einer Wirksamkeitsüberprüfung der Methode.* GRIN Verlag.

Duell, H. (1981). Angreiferverhalten: Bewußt statt zufällig. In H. Duell, W. Eyßer & D. Späte (Hrsg.), *Situationsgerechtes Entscheidungsverhalten im Angriff. Handball Spezial Band 2* (p 13-36). Philippka.

Duell, H., Eyßer, W. & Späte, D. (Eds.). *Situationsgerechtes Entscheidungsverhalten im Angriff. Handball Spezial Band 2.* Philippka.

Eisele, A. (1997). Ablegeball. In S. König & A. Eisele (Hrsg.), *Handball unterrichten* (p 49-52). Hofmann.

Ekblom, B. (1986). Applied physiology of soccer. *Sports Medicine, 3*, 50-60.

Emrich, A. (2016). *Spielend Handball lernen: in Schule und Verein. 7.*, korrigierte Auflage. Limpert.

Engle, R. W. (2002). Working memory capacity as executive attention. Current directions. *Psychological Science, 11*(1), 19-23.

Ericsson, K. A., Krampe, R. T., & Tesch-Römer, C. (1993). The role of deliberative practice in the acquisition of expert performance. *Psychological Review, 100*, 363-406.

Eriksen, C. W., & St. James, J. D. (1986). Visual attention within and around the field of focal attention: A zoom lens model. *Perception & Psychophysics, 40*, 225-240. https://doi.org/10.3758/BF03211502

Farrow, D., & Abernethy, B. (2002). Can anticipatory skills be learned through implicit video-based perceptual training? *Journal of Sports Science, 20*, 471-485.

Fink, A., Rominger, C., Benedek, M., Perchtold, C. M., Papousek, I., Weiss, E. M., Seidel, A., & Memmert, D. (2018). EEG alpha activity during imagining creative moves in soccer decision-making situations. *Neuropsychologia, 114*, 118-124.

Florkiewicz, B., Fogtman, S., Kszak-Krzyżanowska, A., & Zwierko, T. (2014). The ability to maintain attention during visuomotor task performance in handball players and non-athletes. *Central European Journal of Sport Sciences and Medicine, 7*, 99-106.

Friedman, N. P., Miyake, A., Corley, R. P., Young, S. E., DeFries, J. C., & Hewitt, J. K. (2006). Not all executive functions are related to intelligence. *Psychological Science, 17*, 172-179.

Friedrich, W. (2005). *Optimales Sportwissen.* Spitta Verlag GmbH & Co. KG.

Fruchart, E., Pâques, P., & Mullet, E. (2010). Decision-making in basketball and handball games: A developmental perspective. *European Review of Applied Psychology, 60*(1), 27-34.

Memmert, D. & Furley, P. (2007). "I spy with my little eye!" - Breadth of Attention, Inattentional Blindness, and Tactical Decision Making in Team Sports. *Journal of Sport & Exercise Psychology, 29*, 365-347.

Furley, P., & Memmert, D. (2009). Aufmerksamkeitstraining im Sportspiel. *Leistungssport, 3*, 33-36.

Furley, P., & Memmert, D. (2010). The role of working memory in sports. *International Review of Sport and Exercise Psychology, 3*, 171-194.

Furley, P., & Memmert, D. (2012). Working memory capacity as controlled attention in tactical decision making. *Journal of Sport and Exercise Psychology, 34*(3), 322-344.

Furley, P., & Memmert, D. (2013). "Whom should I pass to?" The more options the more attentional guidance from working. *PLOS ONE 8*: e62278. https://doi.org/10.1371/journal.pone.0062278

Furley, P., & Memmert, D. (2015). Creativity and working memory capacity in sports: Working memory capacity is not a limiting factor in creative decision making amongst skilled performers. *Frontiers in Psychology.* https://doi.org/10.3389/fpsyg.2015.00115

Furley, P., Memmert, D., & Heller, C. (2010). The dark side of visual awareness in sport - inattentional blindness in a real-world basketball task. *Attention, Perception & Psychophysics, 72*, 1327-1337.

Furley, P., Memmert, D., & Schmid, S. (2013). Perceptual load in sport and the heuristic value of the perceptual load paradigm in examining expertise-related perceptual-cognitive adaptations. *Cognitive Processing, 14*, 31-42.

Furley, P., Schul, K., & Memmert, D. (2017). Das Experten-Novizen-Paradigma und die Vertrauenskrise in der Psychologie. *Zeitschrift für Sportpsychologie, 23*, 131-140. https://doi.org/10.1026/1612-5010/a000174

Gredin, N. V., Bishop, D. T., Williams, A. M., & Broadbent, D. P. (2020). The use of contextual priors and kinematic information during anticipation in sport: Toward a Bayesian integration framework. *International Review of Sport and Exercise Psychology*, 1-25. https://doi.org/10.1080/1750984X.2020.1855667

Guilford, J. P. (1967). *The nature of human intelligence*. McGraw-Hill.

Güldenpenning, I., Braun, J. F., Machlitt, D., & Schack, T. (2015). Masked priming of complex movements: perceptual and motor processes in unconscious action perception. *Psychological Research, 79*, 801-812.

Güldenpenning, I., Kunde, W., & Weigelt, M. (2017). How to trick your opponent: A review article on deceptive actions in interactive sports. *Frontier in Psychology, 8*, 917.

Güldenpenning, I., Machlitt, D., & Schack, T. (2011). Die unbewusste Wahrnehmung einer Wurftäuschung im Handball. *Beiträge zur 53. Tagung experimentell arbeitender Psychologen (TEAP)*.

Güldenpenning, I., Steinke, A., Koester, D., & Schack, T. (2013). Athletes and novices are differently capable to recognize feint and non-feint actions. *Experimental Brain Research, 230*, 333-343.

Gutiérrez-Aguilar, Ó., Montoya-Fernández, M., Fernández-Romero, J. J., & Saavedra-García, A. M. (2016). Analysis of time-out use in handball and its influence on the game performance. *International Journal of Performance Analysis in Sport, 16*(1), 1-11.

Gutierrez-Davila, M., Rojas, F. J., Ortega, M., Campos, J., & Parraga, J. (2011). Anticipatory strategies of team-handball goalkeepers. *Journal of Sports Sciences, 29*(12), 1321-1328.

Hagemann, N., & Loffing, F. (2013). Antizipation. In A. Güllich & M. Krüger (Eds.), *Sport. Das Lehrbuch für das Sportstudium* (pp. 562-564). Springer.

Hagemann, N., & Memmert, D. (2006). Coaching anticipatory skill in badminton: Laboratory-versus field-based perceptual training? *Journal of Human Movements Studies, 50*, 381-398.

Hambrick, D. Z., & Meinz, E. J. (2011). Limits on the predictive power of domain-specific experience and knowledge in skilled performance. *Current Directions in Psychological Science, 20*, 275-279.

Hambrick, D. Z., Burgoyne, A. P., & Oswald, F. L. (2019). Domain-general models of expertise: The role of cognitive ability. In P. Ward, J. M. Schraagen, J. Gore, & E. Roth (Eds.), *Oxford handbook of expertise: Research and application* (pp. 56-84). Oxford UP.

Hansen, C., Sanz-Lopez, F., Whiteley, R., Popovic, N., Ahmed, H. A., & Cardinale, M. (2017). Performance analysis of male handball goalkeepers at the World Handball championship 2015. *Biology of Sport, 34*(4), 393.

Harris, D., Wilson, M. R., & Vine, S. J. (2018). A systematic review of commercial cognitive training devices: Implications for use in sport. *Frontiers in Psychology, 9*, 709.

Herzog, H. D. (1986). Zur Theoriearbeit im taktischen Training der Sportspiele. *Wissenschaftliche Zeitschrift der DHfK Leipzig, 27*, 73-84.

Hoffmann, E. (1997). Vom Aufsetzerball und Tigerball zum Handball 4 plus 1. In S. König & A. Eisele (Hrsg.), *Handball unterrichten* (S. 56-64). Hofmann.

Hohmann, A., & Pietzonka, M. (2017). *Techniktraining zur Entwicklung der Spielfähigkeit im Fußball, Handball und Basketball* (p. 01). Sportverlag Strauß.

Höner, O. (2005). Entscheidungshandeln im Sportspiel Fußball. *Eine Analyse im Lichte der Rubikon-theorie*. Hofmann.

Hossein, S. M., Mehdi, R., & Mohammad, J. V. (2018). The effect of two months of handball training on the creativity of male students aged 7 to 8 in Dezful. *Journal of Motor and Behavioral Sciences, 1*(3), 183-195.

Hüttermann, S., Memmert, D., Simons, D. J., & Bock, O. (2013). Fixation strategy influences the ability to focus attention on two spatially separate objects. *PLoS ONE, 8*, e65673.

Hüttermann, S., Noël, B., & Memmert, D. (2018). Eye tracking in high-performance sports: Evaluation of its application in expert athletes. *International Journal of Computer Science in Sport, 17*, 182-203.

Hüttermann, S., Simons, D., & Memmert, D. (2014). The size and shape of the attentional "spotlight" varies with differences in sports expertise. *Journal of Experimental Psychology: Applied, 20*, 147-157.

Intriligator, J., & Cavanagh, P. (2001). The spatial resolution of visual attention. *Cognitive psychology, 43*, 171-216.

Jackson, R. C., & Farrow, D. (2005). Implicit perceptual training: How, when and why? *Human Movement Science, 24*, 308-325.

Jackson, R. C., Warren, S., & Abernethy, B. (2006). Anticipation skill and susceptibility to deceptive movements. *Acta Psychology, 123*, 355-371.

Jarraya, M., Jarraya, S., Chtourou, H., Souissi, N., & Chamari, K. (2013). The effect of partial sleep deprivation on the reaction time and the attentional capacities of the handball goalkeeper. *Biological Rhythm Research, 44*(3), 503-510.

Kane, M. J., Hambrick, D. Z., Tuholski, S. W., Wilhelm, O., Payne, T. W., & Engle, R. W. (2004). The generality of working memory capacity: A latent-variable approach to verbal and visuospatial memory span and reasoning. *Journal of Experimental Psychology: General, 133*, 189.

Kelly, M. E., Loughrey, D., Lawlor, B. A., Robertson, I. H., Walsh, C., & Brennan, S. (2014). The impact of cognitive training and mental stimulation on cognitive and everyday functioning of healthy older adults: A systematic review and meta-analysis. *Ageing Research Reviews, 15*, 28–43.

Kempe, M. & Memmert, D. (2018). "Good, better, creative": The influence of creativity on goal scoring in elite soccer. *Journal of Sports Sciences*, 36(3) 1–5.

Kiss, B., & Balogh, L. (2019). A study of key cognitive skills in handball using the Vienna test system. *Journal of Physical Education and Sport, 19*(1), 733-741.

Kempe, M., & Memmert, D. (2018). "Good, better, creative": The influence of creativity on goal scoring in elite soccer. *Journal of Sports Sciences, 36(21)*, 2419–2423

Kleine, T., & Kethorn, J. (2015). Handball-Vermittlung an Hochschulen–ein Multiplikator für die Mitgliederentwicklung und bindung. *Handball-Vermittlung an Hochschulen-ein Multiplikator für die Mitgliederentwicklung und-bindung?! Forschungsprojekt der Projektgruppe „Handball an Hochschulen "im Deutschen Handballbund.* Klingberg, T. (2010). Training and plasticity of working memory. *Trends in Cognitive Sciences, 14*, 317-324.

Knobloch, I., Pieper, M., & Uhrmeister, J. (2020). *Ballschule Handball.* Hofmann.

Knudsen, E. (2007). Fundamental components of attention. Annual Review of Neuroscience, 30, 57–78.

König, H., Greve, S., & Kromer, A. (2018). Handball. *Grundlagen Sport und Sportwissenschaft. Springer VS.*

König, S. & Zentgraf, K. (1997). "Transition" – Spiel- und Übungsformen zum Gegenstoß. In S. König & A. Eisele (Eds.), Handball unterrichten (S. 120–132). Hofmann.

König, S. (1991). *Bewegerentscheidungen im Sportspiel. Eine Untersuchung zur Umsetzung angriffstaktischer Möglichkeiten.* Dissertation. Fakultät für Sozial- und Verhaltenswissenschaften. Selbstverlag.

König, S. (1997). Zur Vermittlung von Spielfähigkeit in der Schule. *Sportunterricht, 46*, 476–486.

König, S., & Husz, A. (2011). *Doppelstunde Handball*. Hofmann.

König, S., & Memmert, D. (2019). Taktik und Taktiktraining im Sport - Anwendungsbereiche, Diagnostik, Trainingsformen, Organisation, Methoden, Anpassungen. In M. Fröhlich & A. Güllich (Eds.), *Sportmotorik, Bewegung und Training*. Springer.

Konzag, I., & Konzag, G. (1980). Anforderungen an die kognitiven Funktionen in der psychischen Regulation sportlicher Spielhandlungen. *Theorie und Praxis der Körperkultur, 29*, 20-31.

Krawczyk, P., Bodasinski, S., Bodasinska, A. & Slupczynski, B. (2018). Level of psychomotor abilities in handball goalkeepers. *Journal of Health and Physical Activity, 10*, 64-71.

Kredel, R., Vater, C., Klostermann, A., & Hossner, E. (2017). Eye-tracking technology and the dynamics of natural gaze behavior in sports: A systematic review of 40 years of research. *Frontiers in Psychology, 8*, 1-15.

Kröger, C., & Miethling, W.D. (2020). Biographische Entwicklungen von Sportspielern - eine explorative Interviewstudie mit aktuellen Spitzenspielern im Fußball und Handball. *German Journal of Exercise and Sport Research, 50*, 534-543.

Kröger, C., & Roth, K. (1999). *Ballschule. Ein ABC für Spielanfänger.* Hoffmann.

Kuhlmann, D. (1998). Wie führt man Spiele ein? In Bielefelder Sportpädagogen (Hrsg.), *Methoden im Sportunterricht* (S. 135-147). Hofmann.

LaBerge, D. (1983). Spatial extent of attention to letters and words. *Journal of Experimental Psychology: Human Perception and Performance, 9*, 371-379.

Lames, M., Dreckmann, C., & Görsdorf, K. (2010). Qualitative Spielbeobachtung im Handball. In *BISp-Jahrbuch, Forschungsförderung 2008/09* (pp. 189-192). BISp.

Lampit, A., Hallock, H., & Valenzuela, M. (2014). Computerized cognitive training in cognitively healthy older adults: A systematic review and meta-analysis of effect modifiers. *PLoS medicine, 11*, e1001756.

Le Menn, M., Bossard, C., Travassos, B., Duarte, R., & Kermarrec, G. (2019). Handball Goalkeeper Intuitive Decision-Making: A Naturalistic Case Study. *Journal of Human Kinetics, 70*(1), 297-308.

Lidor, R., Argov, E., & Daniel, S. (1998). An exploratory study of perceptual-motor abilities of women: Novice and skilled players of team handball. *Perceptual and Motor Skills, 86*(1), 279-288.

Loffing, F. (2017). *Eye-Tracking im Spitzensport-Validität, Grenzen und Möglichkeiten.* Sportverlag Strauß.

Loffing, F., & Cañal-Bruland, R. (2017). Anticipation in sport. *Current Opinion in Psychology, 16*, 6–11.

Loffing, F., & Hagemann, N. (2014). Skill differences in visual anticipation of type of throw in team-handball penalties. *Psychology of Sport and Exercise, 15*(3), 260–267.

Loffing, F., Cañal-Bruland, R., & Hagemann, N. (2014). Antizipationstraining im Sport. In K. Zentgraf & J. Munzert (Eds.). *Kognitives Training im Sport* (pp. 137–161). Hogrefe.

Loffing, F., Hagemann, N., & Farrow, D. (2017). Perceptual-cognitive training: The next piece of the puzzle. In J. Baker, S. Cobley, J. Schorer, & N. Wattie (Eds.), *Routledge handbook of talent identification and development in sport* (pp. 207–220). Routledge.

Loffing, F., Sölter, F., Hagemann, N., & Strauss, B. (2015). Accuracy of outcome anticipation, but not gaze behavior, differs against left-and right-handed penalties in team-handball goalkeeping. *Frontiers in Psychology, 6*, 1820.

Luciana, M., Conklin, H. M., Hooper, C. J., & Yarger, R. S. (2005). The development of nonverbal working memory and executive control processes in adolescents. *Child Development, 76*, 697–712.

Mack, A., & Rock, I. (1998). *Inattentional blindness.* MIT Press.

Macnamara, B. N., Hambrick, D. Z., & Oswald, F. L. (2014). Deliberate practice and performance in music, games, sports, education, and professions: A meta-analysis. *Psychological Science, 25*, 1608–1618.

Madou, K. H. (2020). Physical demands and physiological aspects in elite team handball in Germany and Switzerland: An analysis of the game. *MOJ Sports Med, 4*(3), 55–62.

Magnaguagno, L., & Hossner, E.-J. (2020). The impact of self-generated and explicitly acquired contextual knowledge on anticipatory performance. *Journal of Sports Sciences, 38*(18), 2108–2117.

Mann, D. L., Schaefers, T., & Cañal-Bruland, R. (2014). Action preferences and the anticipation of action outcomes. *Acta Psychologica, 152*, 1–9.

Mann, D. T., Williams, A. M., Ward, P., & Janelle, C. M. (2007). Perceptual-cognitive expertise in sport: A meta-analysis. *Journal of Sport & Exercise Psychology. 29*, 457–478.

Marr, D. (1982). *Vision: A computational investigation into the human representation and processing of visual information.* Freeman.

Masters, R. S. W., van der Kamp, J., & Jackson, R. C. (2007). Imperceptibly off-center goalkeepers influence penalty-kick direction in soccer. *Psychological Science, 18*, 222–223.

Maxwell, J. P., Masters, R. S., & Eves, F. F. (2003). The role of working memory in motor learning and performance. *Consciousness and Cognition, 12*, 376-402.

Memmert, D. & König, S. (2012). Zur Vermittlung einer allgemeinen Spielfähigkeit im Sportspiel. In S. König, D. Memmert, & K. Moosmann (Eds.), *Das große Buch der Sportspiele* (pp. 18-37). Limpert-Verlag.

Memmert, D. (2004a). *Kognitionen im Sportspiel.* Sport & Buch Strauß.

Memmert, D. (2004b). Ein Forschungsprogramm zur Validierung sportspielübergreifender Basistaktiken. *Sportwissenschaft, 34*(3), 341-354.

Memmert, D. (2005). Ich sehe was, was du nicht siehst! - Das Phänomen Inattentional Blindness im Sport. *Leistungssport, 35*(5), 11-15.

Memmert, D. (2006). Wann soll man spezialisieren? - Kreativität als Indikator auf der 1. und 2. Stufe des MSIL. In K. Weber, D. Augustin, P. Maier, & K. Roth (Eds.). *Wissenschaftlicher Transfer für die Praxis: Ausbildung - Training - Wettkampf* (pp. 59-64). Sport & Buch Strauß.

Memmert, D. (2007). Can creativity be improved by an attention-broadening training program?-An exploratory study focusing on team sports. *Creativity Research Journal, 19*(2-3), 281-291.

Memmert, D. (2009). Pay attention! A review of attentional expertise in sport. *International Review of Sport & Exercise Psychology, 2*(2), 119-138.

Memmert, D. (2010a). Creativity, expertise, and attention: Exploring their development and their relationships. *Journal of Sport Science, 29*(1), 93-104.

Memmert, D. (2010b). Testing of tactical performance in youth elite soccer. Journal of *Sports Science & Medicine, 9*(2), 199-205.

Memmert, D. (2012). Kreativität im Sportspiel. *Sportwissenschaft, 42*(1), 38-49.

Memmert, D. (2013). Leistungsfaktoren im Sportspiel. In A. Güllich & M. Krüger (Eds.), *Sport - Das Lehrbuch für das Sportstudium* (pp. 561-562). Springer Verlag.

Memmert, D. (2015a). *Teaching tactical creativity in team and racket sports: Research and practice*. Routledge.

Memmert, D. (2015b). Visual Attention in Sports. In J. Fawcett, E. F. Risko, & A. Kingstone (Eds.), *The Handbook of Attention* (pp. 643-662). MIT Press.

Memmert, D. (2017a). Tactical creativity in sport. In J. Kaufman, V. Glăveanu, & J. Baer (Eds.), *The Cambridge handbook of creativity across domains* (pp. 479-491). Cambridge University Press. Hhttps://doi.org/10.1017/9781316274385.026

Memmert, D. (2019). *Fußballspiele werden im Kopf entschieden*. Meyer & Meyer.

Memmert, D., & Breihofer, P. (2006). *Doppelstunde Handball*. Hofmann.

Memmert, D., & Furley, P. (2007). "I spy with my little eye!"-Breadth of attention, inattentional blindness, and tactical decision making in team sports. *Journal of Sport & Exercise Psychology, 29*(3), 365-347.

Memmert, D., & Furley, P. (2012). Aufmerksamkeit. In M. Krüger & A. Güllich (Eds.), Bachelor-Kurs Sport. *Ein Lehrbuch für das Studium der Sportwissenschaft* (pp. 567-568). Springer.

Memmert, D., & Roth, K. (2003). Individualtaktische Leistungsdiagnostik im Sportspiel. *Spektrum der Sportwissenschaft, 15*, 44-70.

Memmert, D., & Roth, K. (2007). The effects of non-specific and specific concepts on tactical creativity in team ball sports. *Journal of Sports Sciences, 25*(12), 1423-1432.

Memmert, D., Baker, J., & Bertsch, C. (2010). Play and practice in the development of sport-specific creativity in team ball sports. *High Ability Studies, 21*, 3-18.

Memmert, D., Hagemann, H., Althoetmar, R. Geppert, S., & Seiler, D. (2009). Conditions of practice in perceptual skill learning. *Research Quarterly for Exercise & Sport, 80*, 32-43. https://doi.org/10.1080/02701367.2009.10599527

Memmert, D., Hüttermann, S., & Kreitz, C. (2019). Wahrnehmung und Aufmerksamkeit. In J. Schüler, M. Wegner, & H. Plessner (Eds.), *Lehrbuch Sportpsychologie - Theoretische Grundlagen und Anwendung* (pp. 13-41). Springer.

Memmert, D., Hüttermann, S., & Orliczek, J. (2013). Decide like Lionel Messi! The impact of regulatory focus on divergent thinking in ports. *Journal of Applied Social Psychology, 43*, 2163-2167.

Memmert, D., Thumfart, M., & Uhing, M. (2014). Optimales Taktiktraining im Kinder-, *Jugend- und Leistungshandball*. Spitta Verlag.

Mirsky, A. F., Anthony, B. J., Duncan, C. C, Ahearn, M. B., & Kellam, S. G. (1991). Analysis of the elements of attention: A neuropsychological approach. *Neuropsychological Review, 2*, 109-145.

Mohammed, D. S., & Abdullah, A. A. Z. (2018). Effect of educational exercises with (Cogni Plus) in focusing attention and some forms of correction in students' handball. *Al. Qadisiya journal for the Sciences of Physical Education, 18*(2). 25–30.

Moran, A. P. (1996). *The psychology of concentration in sport performers: A cognitive analysis*. Psychology Press.

Morillo, J. P., Reigal, R. E., Hernández-Mendo, A., Montaña, A., & Morales-Sánchez, V. (2017). Decision-making by handball referees: design of an ad hoc observation instrument and polar coordinate analysis. *Frontiers in Psychology, 8*, 1842.

Most, S. B., Scholl, B. J., Clifford, E. R., & Simons, D. J. (2005). What you see is what you set: Sustained inattentional blindness and the capture of awareness. *Psychological Review, 112*, 217–242.

Neisser, U. (2014). *Cognitive psychology* (Classic edition). Psychology Press.

Noël, B., van der Kamp, J., & Memmert, D. (2015). Implicit goalkeeper influences on goal side selection in representative penalty kicking tasks. *PLoS ONE, 10*, e01354423.

Noël, B., van der Kamp, J., Masters, R., & Memmert, D. (2016). Scan direction influences explicit but not implicit perception of a goalkeeper's position. *Attention, Perception & Psychophysics*. doi: 10.3758/s13414-016-1196-2

Noël, B., van der Kamp, J., Weigelt, M., & Memmert, D. (2015). Asymmetries in spatial perception are more prevalent under explicit than implicit attention. *Consciousness and Cognition, 34*, 10–15.

North, J. S., Ward, P., Ericsson, A., & Williams, A. M. (2011). Mechanisms underlying skilled anticipation and recognition in a dynamic and temporally constrained domain. *Memory 19*, 155–168.

Ohlert, J., & Kleinert, J. (2014). Entwicklungsaufgaben jugendlicher Elite-Handballerinnen und -Handballer. *Zeitschrift für Sportpsychologie, 21*, 161-172.

Olivier, N. (1996). *Techniktraining unter konditioneller Belastung*. Hofmann

Owen, A. M., Hampshire, A., Grahn, J. A., Stenton, R., Dajani, S., Burns, A. S., Howard. R., & Ballard, C. G. (2010). Putting brain training to the test. *Nature, 465*, 775–778.

Pietro, M. (2018). Monitoring and upgrading of coordinative and conditional capacities of young athletes practicing handball. *Journal of Physical Education and Sport, 18*, 465-468.

Posner, M. I. (1980). Orienting of attention. *Quarterly Journal of Experimental Psychology, 32*, 3–25. https://doi.org/10.1080/00335558008248231

Posner, M. I., & Boies, S. J. (1971). *Components of attention. Psychological Review, 78*, 391-408.

Posner, M. I., & Peterson, S. E. (1990). The attention system of the human brain. *Annual Review of Neuroscience, 13*, 25-42. https://doi.org/10.1146/annurev.ne.13.030190.000325

Prinz, W. (1997). Perception and action planning. European Journal of Cognitive *Psychology, 9*(2), 129-154. https://doi.org/10.1080/713752551

Raab, M. (2001). *SMART. Techniken des Taktiktrainings. Taktiken des Techniktrainings.* Strauß.

Raab, M., Zastrow, H., & Häger, J. (2008). Entwicklung eines Messplatztrainings für taktische Kompetenzen im Handball (pp. 201-204). BISp-Jahrbuch - Forschungsförderung 2008/09. BISp Bonn.

Raab, M., Zastrow, H., & Lempertz, C. (2007). *Wege zur Spielintelligenz.* Sportverlag Strauß.

Rojas, F. J., Gutiérrez-Davila, M., Ortega, M., Campos, J., & Párraga, J. (2012). Biomechanical analysis of anticipation of elite and inexperienced goalkeepers to distance shots in handball. *Journal of Human Kinetics, 34*(1), 41-48.

Romeas, T., Guldner, A., & Faubert, J. (2016). 3D-multiple object tracking training task improves passing decision-making accuracy in soccer players. *Psychology of Sport and Exercise, 22*, 1-9.

Rominger, C., Koschutnig, K, Memmert, D., Papousek, I., Perchtold-Stefan C. M., Bendeck, M., Schwertfeder, A. R., & Fink, A. (2021). Brain activation during the observation of real soccer game situations predicts creative goal scoring. *Social Cognitive and Affective Neuroscience, 16*(7), 707-715. https://doi.org/10.1093/scan/nsab035

Rominger, C., Koschutnig, K., Memmert, D., Papousek, I., Perchtold-Stefan, C. M., Benedek, M., ... & Fink, A. (2021). Brain activation during the observation of real soccer game situations predicts creative goal scoring. Social Cognitive and Affective Neuroscience, 16(7), 707-715.

Rominger, C., Memmert, D., Papousek, I., Perchtold-Stefan, C. M., Weiss, E. M., Benedek, M., Schwerdtfeger, A. R., & Fink, A. (2020). Different neurocognitive strategies in women and men in generating creative solutions in soccer decision-making situations. *Psychology of Sport & Exercise, 50* [101748]. https://doi.org/10.1016/j.psychsport.2020.101748

Roth, G., & Menzel, R. (2001). Neuronale Grundlagen kognitiver Leistungen. In J. Dudel, R. Menzel, & R. F. Schmidt (Eds.), *Neurowissenschaft. Vom Molekül zur Kognition* (pp. 543–563). Springer.

Roth, K. (1989). *Taktik im Sportspiel: zum Erklärungswert der Theorie generalisierter motorischer Programme für die Regulation komplexer Bewegungshandlungen.* Hofmann.

Roth, K. (2005). Taktiktraining. In A. Hohmann, M. Kolb, & K. Roth (Eds.), *Handbuch Sportspiel* (pp. 342–349). Hofmann.

Roth, K., & Hossner, E. J. (1999). Die funktionalen Betrachtungsweisen. In K. Roth & K. Willimczik (Eds.), *Bewegungswissenschaft* (pp. 127–225). Rowohlt.

Roth, K., & Kröger, C. (2011). *Ballschule. Ein ABC für Spielanfänger* (4. Aufl.). Hofmann.

Roth, K., Damm, T., Pieper, M., & Roth, C. (2014). *Ballschule in der Primarstufe. 26 komplette Unterrichtseinheiten für die Klassen 1 bis 4*. Hofmann.

Roth, K., Kröger, C., & Memmert, D. (2002). *Ballschule Rückschlagspiele*. Hofmann.

Roth, K., Memmert, D., & Schubert, R. (2006). *Ballschule Wurfspiele*. Hofmann.

Ruß, N. (2020). *Entwicklung einer taktischen Leistungsdiagnostik im Handball für den E- und D-Jugendbereich* (unveröffentlichte Zulassungsarbeit). Ruprecht-Karls-Universität Heidelberg.

Santos, S. D., Memmert, D., Sampaio, J., & Leite, N. (2016). The spawns of creative behavior in team sports: A creativity developmental framework. *Frontiers in Psychology, 7*, 1282.

Sarrazin, P., Vallerand, R., Guillet, E., Pelletier, L., & Cury, F. (2002). Motivation and dropout in female handballers: A 21-month prospective study. *European Journal of Social Psychology, 32*(3), 395–418.

Scharfen, H.-E., & Memmert, D. (2019a). Measurement of cognitive functions in experts and elite-athletes: A meta-analytic review. *Applied Cognitive Psychology, 1–18. DOI:10.1002/acp.3526*

Scharfen, H.-E. & Memmert, D. (2019b). The relationship between cognitive functions and sport-specific motor skills in elite youth soccer players. *Frontiers in Psychology–Movement Science & Sport Psychology, 10*, 817. https://doi.org/10.3389/fpsyg.2019.00817

Scharfen, H.-E., & Memmert, D. (2021). Cognitive training in elite soccer players: evidence of narrow, but not broad transfer to visual and executive function. *German Journal of Exercise and Sport Research, 51*(2), 1–11.

Schmidt, R. A., & Wrisberg, C. A. (2004). *Motor learning and performance. A problem-based learning approach* (3rd ed.). Human Kinetics.

Schorer, J., Faber, I., Koopmann, T., Büsch, D., & Baker, J. (2020). Predictive value of coaches' early technical and tactical notational analyses on long-term success of female handball players. *Journal of Sports Sciences, 38*(19), 2208-2214. https://doi.org/10.1080/02640414.2020.1776923

Schorer, J., Heibuelt, N., Wilson, S. G., & Loffing, F. (2021). Sleep facilitates anticipation training of a handball goalkeeping task in novices. *Psychology of Sport and Exercise, 53*, 101841.

Schorer, J., Panten, J., Neugebauer, J., & Loffing, F. (2018). Perceptual expertise in handball. *In Handball Sports Medicine* (pp. 597-614). Springer.

Sebanz, N., & Shiffrar, M. (2009). Detecting deception in a bluffing body: The role of expertise. *Psychonomic Bulletin & Review, 16*, 170-175.

Shao, Y. K., Mang, J., Li, P. L., Wang, J., Deng, T., & Xu, Z. X. (2015). Computer-based cognitive programs for improvement of memory, processing speed and executive function during age-related cognitive decline: a meta-analysis. *PloS one, 10*, e0130831.

Sichelschmidt, P., Eyßer, W., & Späte, D. (1988). *Entscheidungstraining für Angreifer.* Philippka.

Simons, D. J., Boot, W. R., Charness, N., Gathercole, S. E., Chabris, C. F., Hambrick, D. Z., & Stine-Morrow, E. A. (2016). Do "brain-training" programs work? *Psychological Science in the Public Interest, 17*, 103-186.

Smeeton, N. J., & Williams, A. M. (2012). The role of movement exaggeration in the anticipation of deceptive soccer penalty kicks. *British Journal of Psychology, 103*, 539-555.

Spencer, M. R., & Gastin, P. B. (2001). Energy system contribution during 200-to 1500-m running in highly trained athletes. *Medicine & Science in Sport & Exercise, 33*, 157-162.

Stiehler, G., Konzag, I., & Döbler, H. (1988). *Sportspiele. Theorie und Methodik der Sportspiele. Basketball - Handball - Handball - Volleyball.* Sportverlag.

Strykalenko, Y., Shalar, O., Huzar, V., Voloshinov, S., Yuskiv, S., Silvestrova, H., & Holenko, N. (2020). The correlation between intelligence and competitive activities of elite female handball players. *Journal of Physical Education & Sport, 20*(1). 6-70.

Styles, E. A. (2008). *The psychology of attention.* Psychology Press.

Tanggaard, L., Laursen, D. N., & Szulevicz, T. (2016). The grip on the handball-a qualitative analysis of the influence of materiality on creativity in sport. Qualitative Research in Sport. *Exercise and Health, 8*(1), 79-94.

Tenenbaum, G. (2003). Expert athletes: An integrated approach to decision making. In J. L. Starkes & K. A. Ericsson (Eds.), *Expert performance in sports* (pp. 191-218). Human Kinetics.

Thienes, G. (2019). Schnelligkeit. In A. Güllich & M. Krüger (Eds.), *Bewegung, Training, Leistung und Gesundheit.* https://doi.org/10.1007/978-3-662-53386-4_48-1

Toril, P., Reales, J. M., & Ballesteros, S. (2014). Video game training enhances cognition of older adults: a meta-analytic study. *Psychology and Aging, 29*, 706.

van Zomeren, A. H., & Brouwer, W. H. (1994). *Clinical neuropsychology of attention.* University Press.

Verburgh, L., Scherder, E. J., Van Lange, P. A., & Oosterlaan, J. (2016). Do elite and amateur soccer players outperform non-athletes on neurocognitive functioning? A study among 8-12 years old children. *PloS One, 11*, e:0165741. https://doi.org/10.1371/journal.pone.0165741

Vestberg, T., Gustafson, R., Maurex, L., Ingvar, M., & Petrovic, P. (2012). Executive functions predict the success of top-soccer players. *PloS one, 7*, e34731. https://doi.org/10.1371/journal.pone.0034731

Voss, M. W., Kramer, A. F., Basak, C., Prakash, R. S., & Roberts, B. (2010). Are expert athletes "expert" in the cognitive laboratory? A meta-analytic review of cognition and sport expertise. *Applied Cognitive Psychology, 24*(6), 812-826.

Wagner, H., Finkenzeller, T., Würth, S., & Von Duvillard, S. P. (2014). Individual and team performance in team-handball: A review. *Journal of Sports Science & Medicine, 13*(4), 808.

Wegner, M. & Katzenberger, C. (1994). Die Spielkonzeption zur Lösung taktischer Problemsituationen: Wissenschaftliche Fundierung eines Trainingsprogramms zum Gegenstoßverhalten im Handball. In R. Brack, A. Hohmann, & H. Wieland (Eds.), *Trainingssteuerung* (pp. 248-253). Naglschmid.

Weigel, P. (2018). Decision-Making in Modern Handball. In L. Laver, P. Landreau, R. Seil, & N. Popovic (Eds.). *Handball Sports Medicine: Basic science, injury management and return to sport* (pp. 627-637). Heidelberg.

Weigelt, M., Memmert, D., & Schack, T. (2012). Kick it like Ballack: The effects of goalkeeping gestures on goal-side selection in experienced soccer players and soccer novices. *Journal of Cognitive Psychology, 24*, 942-956.

Weyermann, E. & König, S. (2021). Effects of bilateral exercises in youths' handball-A research programme in progress. In EHF (Ed.), Digitalization and Technology in Handball - Natural Sciences/The Game/Humanities. 6th EHF Scientific Conference, November, 4th-5th, 2021 (pp. 166-172). European Handball Federation.

Williams, A. M., & Ericsson, K. A. (2005). Some considerations when applying the expert performance approach in sport. *Human Movement Science, 24*, 283-307.

Williams, A. M., & Jackson, R. C. (2019). Anticipation in sport: Fifty years on, what have we learned and what research still needs to be undertaken? *Psychology of Sport and Exercise, 42*, 16-24. https:// 10.1016/j.psychsport.2018.11.014

Williams, A. M., Davids, K., & Williams, J. G. (1999). *Visual perception and action in sport.* E & F.N Spon.

Williams, A. M., Ford, P., Eccles, D. W., & Ward, P. (2010). Perceptual-cognitive expertise in sport and its acquisition: Implications for applied cognitive psychology. *Applied Cognitive Psychology.*

Williams, A. M., Hodges, N.J., North, J. S., & Barton, G. (2006). Perceiving patterns of play in dynamic sport tasks: Identifying the essential information underlying skilled performance. *Perception, 35*(3), 317-332. https://doi.org/10.1068/p5310

Williams, A. M., Ward, P., & Chapman, C. (2003). Training perceptual skill in field hockey: Is there transfer from the laboratory to the field. *Research Quarterly for Exercise & Sport, 74*(1), 98-103.

Williams, A. M., Ward, P., Smeeton, N. J., & Allen, D. (2004). Developing anticipation skills in tennis using on-court instruction: Perception versus perception and action. *Journal of Applied Sport Psychology, 16*(4), 350-360.

Wulf, G. (2007). *Attention and motor skill learning.* Human Kinetics.

About the Authors

Daniel Memmert is a professor and executive head of the Institute of Exercise Training and Sport Informatics at the German Sport University Cologne (https://www.dshs-koeln.de/en/visitenkarte/person/univ-prof-dr-daniel-memmert/). From 2009 to 2016, he was head at the Institute for Cognition and Sports Game Research at the German Sport University Cologne. In 2003, he received his PhD (award: dvs Young Scientist Award, bronze) and, in 2008, qualified for a professorship at the Elite University of Heidelberg (award: DOSB Science Award, bronze). In 2014, he was a visiting professor at the University of Vienna. His scientific work focuses on movement science (cognition and motor function), sports psychology (attention and motivation), and computer science in sports (Big Data, pattern recognition and simulation).

According to a publicly accessible database by Elsevier of the world's top 100,000 scientists (https://data.mendeley.com/datasets/btchxktzyw/2), he ranks first in Germany in the field of Sport Science and eighth in the world in the field of Sports Science/Experimental Psychology. He has an H-index of 63 (i10-index 215) and has raised more than 8 million Euros in third-party funding (e.g., BMBF, BISp), including nine DFG projects in the field of computer science and five DFG projects in the field of psychology. In addition, he has completed several research stays (e.g., USA, Canada), won various awards (e.g., DOSB Science Award Bronze, Research Writing Award AAHPERD), serves on international editorial boards, and has published more than 300 articles in international journals, 35 books, and 35 book chapters. From 2009 to 2013, he was executive director of asp (Association for Sport Psychology); from 2012 to 2016, he was editor of the *Journal of Sport Science* (behavioral science section); from 2016 to 2018, he was associate editor (psychology) for the journal *Research Quarterly for Exercise and Sport*; from 2017 to 2021, he was the associate editor for the *Journal of Sport Psychology;* and from 2009 to 2022, he was deputy speaker of the dvs commission "Team Sports." Currently, he is editor-in-chief for *Journal of Applied Sport and Exercise Psychology* and associate editor for *International Journal of Sport and Exercise Psychology*. He holds coaching licenses in soccer, tennis, snowboarding, as well as alpine skiing, and he is editor and author of textbooks on modern soccer training. His institute has cooperated with various Bundesliga soccer teams, the German national soccer team, and DAX companies and organized the first international master's degree course in Match Analysis.

Prof. Dr. Stefan König is subject spokesman and professor at the Sports Center as well as director of the Research Center for Secondary Education at the Weingarten University of Education. From 1995 to 2006, he was academic director and head of studies at the Institute of Sport Science University of Tübingen. In 1991, he also received his doctorate from the University of Tübingen. His scientific work focuses on training science (effects of training processes in school, recreational, and health sports), school sports research (effects of physical education, school sports concepts, sports teacher research), sports game research (mediation concepts, tactics, leadership behavior), and research methodology (mixed methods research).

He is editor of four book series *(Schulsportforschung, Doppelstunde Sport, Sportstunde Grundschule, Weingartner Dialog uber Forschung)* as well as the journal *SportPraxis*, an ad hoc reviewer for a range of international and national journals, and a reviewer for the *Kooperationsgemeinschaft gesetzlicher Krankenkassen* and the BISP. He has been a member of the WLSB Science Forum since 2015, a board member of the Faculty Association of Sports Science since 2016, a member of the Editorial Board of the *International Journal of Multimethod Research Approaches* since 2017, and a representative in the TGfU Special Interest Group since 2020. He has obtained various third-party funding projects (including IBH, BISP) and collaborates with a variety of sport associations and educational institutions in research projects. He holds coaching licenses in handball and basketball.

Credits

Cover and interior design:	Anja Elsen
Layout:	Anja Elsen, Katerina Georgieva
Cover photo:	© AdobeStock
Interior photos:	© dpa - picture alliance: pp. 13, 23, 39, 77, 135, 141, 157
Interior figures:	© easy sports graphics: pp. 78-167; © Daniel Memmert: pp. 27, 28, 44, 48, 59, 60-65, 67, 70, 72; © König & Husz: pp. 76
Managing editor:	Elizabeth Evans
Copy editor:	Anne Rumery